CO-PARENTING
STRANGERS

CO-PARENTING STRANGERS

*How to find and keep
the very best of childcare providers*

THERESA J. MULHERN

AuthorHouse™
1663 Liberty Drive
Bloomington, IN 47403
www.authorhouse.com
Phone: 1-800-839-8640

© 2013 by Theresa J. Mulhern. All rights reserved.

No part of this book may be reproduced, stored in a retrieval system, or transmitted by any means without the written permission of the author.

Published by AuthorHouse   04/01/2013

ISBN: 978-1-4817-3578-0 (sc)
ISBN: 978-1-4817-3579-7 (hc)
ISBN: 978-1-4817-3580-3 (e)

Library of Congress Control Number: 2013905615

Any people depicted in stock imagery provided by Thinkstock are models, and such images are being used for illustrative purposes only.
Certain stock imagery © Thinkstock.

This book is printed on acid-free paper.

Because of the dynamic nature of the Internet, any web addresses or links contained in this book may have changed since publication and may no longer be valid. The views expressed in this work are solely those of the author and do not necessarily reflect the views of the publisher, and the publisher hereby disclaims any responsibility for them.

Contents

The Primary Caretaker 1
Choosing Your Child's Co-Parent 9
Your Expectations of Childcare 21
When Standard Options Cannot Meet Your Needs 31
When Someone Else Pays the Bill 36
You've made your Choice—Now do the Research 44
Building a Trust Relationship 53
Your Provider's Legal Obligations 63
Your Parental Responsibilities 69
Choosing to hire In-House—The Nanny or Au Pair 79
Daycare Etiquette 84
Addressing Concerns about Care 90
Discipline—The United Front 96
Oh that Pesky Paperwork—What to expect in a contract 99
A Back-up Plan for Sick Days 104
Save the Drama for Your Mama 113
The Child and Adult Food Program 117
Handling Emergencies 121
When to Take Action 127
The Real Cost of Childcare 132
Summing it all up 135

Foreword

27 years ago I began caring for children, starting as a nanny of 3 summers and school breaks. At first it was just a job, even though I loved the kids. It wasn't until I had my first child that I realized just how important the job of childcare is. I was working in corporate America and making a good living. The moment I held my daughter I knew I couldn't trust anyone with her. I knew I would have to figure out a way to be able to stay home, but I couldn't afford to give up my income, which was well above the median.

Shortly after I had my daughter a friend asked if I would watch her 7 year old for the summer break while on maternity leave. Tabitha was my first daycare child and is now in her thirties and I hear she is raising and training horses in Molalla Oregon. Yes, I know where she is, along with a couple dozen other grown adults who came to me as children. Every now and then I will be out in public and have someone come up to me and tell me they used to come to my house as a child. I always feel pride in the adults they have become. Anyway, Tabitha over the summer gave me time to get four more kids by fall, and by Christmas I had 8, which was a full house for the registration hanging on the wall.

It didn't take me long to get hooked. Getting paid to play with play-dough is awesome. I go from bed to the coffee pot and I am at work. I don't buy expensive suits or lunches out anymore. I buy nursing scrubs, because they look good and wash easily. I don't carry a briefcase but I do sport a very stylish baby backpack. Instead of conference calls I have parent conferences and instead of corporate reports I file food program attendance records.

Because of the casual atmosphere a lot of people think my job is a game or a joke. I get referred to as a babysitter and a grandma figure. The

Theresa J. Mulhern

first question I get asked in an interview isn't about my education or experience, but always about my rate, as if bargain basement cost for care is the goal, instead of finding the very best provider out there. Truthfully there have been times that I have gone through phases of giving less than my best simply because I felt that it made no difference to the parents as long as the rate was low. It never took long, however, to snap back to the realization that the parents weren't my clients.

Over the last quarter of a century childcare, parents and children have changed a lot, and not all of it is for the better. This book is my attempt to educate parents about how to find the very best caregiver for their family and how to get only her very best work.

This book was a long time in the making. It was twenty years before I started on this and another four before I was ready to publish it. I owe thanks to so many for their help. Thank-you to my family for giving up a lot of quality time. I also want to thank the childcare families who read and gave reviews on chapters to help me stay on task. Finally I want to thank the employees who forced my daycare centers to close because I wouldn't tolerate apathy, laziness and welfare fraud. Not only did they give me time to finish the book, but they got me back to what I love, which is actually caring for kids. That's another book altogether, called "Work Me / Homie", in case you love this one and can't wait for more. I hope this one helps families everywhere, and makes providers pay attention to how important what we do is.

The Primary Caretaker

If you have opened this book you are one of millions of parents who either are working or are going to start working while your child is under the age of 12. There's no shame in it. Don't ever let anyone tell you that because you choose to work you are cheating your child.

The truth is that with the right amount of effort you can be a great parent who works. It will require a lot of sacrificing on your part. There won't be a lot of volleyball leagues or girl's nights out for a few years, but there might be tea parties and sleepovers and other ways for you to be creative and use some of your hidden talents.

Parenting doesn't just change your schedule, it changes your universe. Some people find they had talents and interests they never knew about. I found out after having a daughter that I love to decorate cakes and bedrooms. I had never cared about either before. In addition my teenagers have taught me a lot about computers and introduced me to contemporary music that doesn't make me feel like screaming and smashing things. I have learned that instead of dinner out I can play restaurant using sandwiches with the crust cut off and tiny little cups of chocolate milk.

I chose to stay home with all of our eight children. In order to still contribute to the family income I decided to do daycare. I had always watched our friend's children for free and had helped raise my younger siblings, nieces and nephews. I think I work harder at home than I ever did in the corporate world. I know I work longer hours for less pay.

But we must get back to the subject at hand. Probably before you had children you chose someone to have them with. Maybe not and if you're doing it on your own then you really have to have a paycheck. But if you are lucky enough to have a significant other chances are good you didn't select them overnight or out of listing of neighborhood available bachelors.

When you choose a life partner you have time to become friends, date and get to know about each other. Before you have children I would hope that you talk about all that you want for them and how you plan on raising them. Will they go to public or private school? Will they be Catholic or Mormon? Will they be able to date at 15 or will they be locked up until 25? You definitely won't agree on everything but at least you have a jumping off point.

Unfortunately, you won't get the same opportunity with your childcare provider. Most people choose a daycare provider within 2 weeks of beginning their search. Imagine if you chose your spouse that way!

Your childcare provider is, next to your immediate family, the most important relationship you will ever have. This is a person who spends 8-12 hours of time with your child every day. They will have more time with your child awake each week than you do, and they will see a lot of firsts that you will miss. There will be times you will be jealous that your child leans out of your arms to go to them, or won't stop staring at them when you arrive and want to be noticed. There will be times you will be angry with them for presuming to tell you about your child. Sometimes you will wonder why they seem to have the magic touch. Your child will be happy for them all day and a crying mess for you all night.

Even after you hire this perfect person, at times you will totally disagree with the way they are raising your child. There will be problems that need addressed. Working out these problems can be a lot like marriage. You will have to learn how to fight fair, only bring up relevant issues and let things go when they are over. The following story illustrates how things can get out of hand with just a simple misunderstanding.

> *My son Nicolais is an avid reader. I have never been able to limit his reading. I would buy books I thought he would like and I would catch him reading my thrillers. I would leave my*

magazines down and he would bring me the latest information on organizing the kitchen (thinking I wanted to be organized).

Being a Mormon household, we don't keep inappropriate materials around. We do however have 8 kids and 4 of them are over the age of 14. Since we don't home school or lock them in the closet I assume they are exposed to things they shouldn't be. I was sure however, that my young children were not being exposed to nudity of any kind.

Confident in my supervisory capacity, I was unprepared for the angry phone call I received from Amy K. at seven on a Thursday night.

"I am truly concerned" Amy began "about Alan and Cindy and what they are being exposed to at your house." She continued "Your seven year old is a little porn king!"

I was immediately offended and upset. "I have no idea what you are talking about" I argued. "My son doesn't have access to any of that kind of material and I am sure you are misinformed."

"I am not misinformed and I feel that I need to give my notice. Alan told me that Nico showed him pictures of boobies while they were playing in his room today. I just want to know, are you even watching these kids?"

I was off the couch and headed for my son's room before she even finished her sentence. When I got there my son was on the floor building with his brother. "Matthew, leave the room so I can speak with Nico" I barked. Normally I would get an argument but he seemed to sense my anxiety. He headed out the door and I confronted my then 8 year old, who was looking at me with a look that clearly shouted 'I have no clue what I did'.

"Nicolais Alexander Mulhern, Have you been showing pictures of naked women to Alan or any of the other children?" At this point I wasn't even sure I wanted an answer. My eyes were scanning the

room looking for copies of Penthouse or Playboy just laying out for the world to see.

"Are you crazy mom?" Nico still looked puzzled and upset "I don't have naked pictures"

Amy was already arguing, obviously able to hear the other side of my conversation with my son. "Alex said it's in a brown book and he has it hidden under his bed." Now I was in a panic. How would she know Nico kept his books in a plastic box under his bed so that he could read at bedtime?

I rushed over and grabbed the tote from under the bed. Without even realizing I was holding my breath I began searching for anything that looked menacing. The books were all the ones from the library and the books I had bought him over the years. I spied a brown cover and dug to get at it. It was an encyclopedia. I looked at Nico and held it up.

My son's face lit with understanding. He began laughing. I was still completely upset and confused. I asked Amy if the book had gold writing on it. She conferred with Alex and replied that it did.

By now Nico had opened the encyclopedia and was pointing to a picture. It was an illustration of the Sphinx. Not being a big follower of all things Egyptian, I didn't even know the Sphinx had boobies. But there they were and I must say she was very well endowed.

Now I was laughing. Amy was on the other end of the phone still going on about how she trusted me to watch her children and that she should contact social services.

"If you'll give me a minute" I giggled, "I can explain." I told her what book it was, and what the picture was of. I then put Nico on the phone and he explained that Alan was asking about the pyramids because of a book Nico read him about Egypt (my son even loves to read to the daycare kids: which is awesome for me!).

He pulled the book about Egypt from his tote and I read the title to Amy.

Nico apologized to Amy if he showed Alan anything he shouldn't have. I then got back on the phone.

"I am sorry if you are upset Amy" I began. I then heard Amy giggling in the background. It was a few moments before either one of us could talk.

"I'm sorry Terri" she began.

I cut her off before she could go any further. "I probably would have been just as upset." I assured her. "I don't know if I would have called your child a porn king, but I would not have been happy. I do have a proposal for you though. If you promise not to believe everything Alan says happens at daycare, I promise not to believe everything he says happens at home."

We hung up after agreeing that everything was settled and no-authorities would need to be involved, (this time . . .)

Even the Sphinx must have been too pornographic for her though. Thanks to the encyclopedia and my son's need to share the knowledge of the universe, I got my two week notice one week later. I never did see DHS on my doorstep. Either they agreed with me that it was no big deal or she didn't bother to call them.

I now have a clause in my handbook that reads "I promise not to believe everything your child says happens at home if you promise not to believe everything they say happens here . . ." Wise words of wisdom for parents and providers alike.

The first step to hiring a co-provider for your children is to look at the different kinds of childcare. These are:

Licensed Centers are commercial buildings where large numbers of children are cared for. Generally children are divided up by their age into separate rooms. The individuals hired to teach are required to meet certain state guidelines. The minimum age is usually 16, and they are required to undergo training to include CPR and 1st Aid within so many months of starting (usually 6). Be very careful about getting caught up in the idea that centers are better because they are bigger, or because of names they use that lead you to believe there is a better caliber of personnel. For example, in some states the Director is the only person in the building required to have any kind of further education than high school. The fact that the caregivers in each room are called teachers does not mean that they have a teaching degree, although it implies it to parents who are uneducated about daycare regulations. If you think that is bad, even preschools in most states don't require teachers to be actual teachers, and they also don't require them to have even the basic CPR and First Aid certification that daycare providers have to maintain.

Registered Childcare Homes are individual people who have decided to care for children in their residence and have agreed to have their information on file with the State. Although anyone doing childcare is subject to being inspected by the Dept. of Human Services, these individuals have decided to register and follow state guidelines. Depending on the level of registration they receive, they have requirements they also have to meet. The minimum age is usually 18 for the basic license and 21 for a bigger license. They are required to be certified in CPR and 1st Aid and are required to complete continuing education classes each year. Iowa, for example requires 12 hours of continuing education for each year.

Non-registered childcare homes are individuals who have not volunteered to let the state know they are doing childcare. The reason for this could be that they are only going to watch one or two children and do not want to deal with the paperwork. It could also be because for whatever reason they feel the state will deny them registration. Some states still require these individuals to meet certain requirements such as CPR and 1st aid. Most states limit the number of children a provider can legally watch without being registered. In Iowa's case the limit is 5 or less, including their own children who are not in school. We have included those numbers in the back of this book. It is very important to ask the right questions if you are even considering using a non-registered home.

Some states do not allowed non-registered homes, it is important to ask and make sure your provider is not doing something illegal.

Family/Friends are another valid option. This can either be a great solution or a true nightmare. Before selecting this option, consider the individual as if you didn't know them. Do they show up for work every day or call off sick? How are they with their children? Also remember that although they love you, they still need paid a fair wage and treated as a professional. Don't assume that your sister won't mind if you are 2 hours late because she loves you. She may want to spend time with her own children. You must always make sure your bill is paid on time if you are using family. Nothing ruins a great relationship faster than arguments over money.

The last option is In-home. This is where you hire a nanny or mother's helper. They are called a Nanny if you work, and they are called a Mother's helper if you stay home but need someone to help with your children while you shop or run errands. This is a great choice for parents who have special needs or are very demanding and require their child be cared for exclusively. Because this relationship is so different, we will not be including it in the chapter on choosing a co-parent. Instead, there is a chapter on hiring in-home help later on in the book. All of the information in this book is relevant no matter what route you choose, because in the end the book is about how to have a great relationship with the other person you are raising your child with, no matter who they end up being or what kind of license they hold.

Let's move on to the selection process. The information in the next chapter is from our point of view. There can be arguments made for each individual kind of daycare. The best way to decide what to do is to look at several examples of canters and in-homes and judge each one for its own pros and cons. There are great and terrible daycares out there. You do really have to be diligent and make sure you are making a choice you are completely comfortable with.

Before you begin the next chapter, get a notebook, a pen and a listing of local daycares. You can use the references in the back of this book to help locate a list of the right kind of daycares to look at. Type a list of all the questions you want to ask and photocopy it for each provider/center you interview. Make copious notes in the margins and spaces about each place you go, and about the provider you speak with. It is very hard to remember how each person answered 20 questions five hours and three providers later.

Choosing Your Child's Co-Parent

If you are expecting a baby, you should begin looking for childcare at least 3 months before your child is born in order to have time to research cost, learn about the daycare laws and regulations in your state and interview at least 10 providers.

If you are already a parent and are returning to work or changing daycares because you are not happy with your current situation, you unfortunately do not have the luxury of time. You do still have a responsibility to interview several providers, which can be done with an initial phone interview and follow up personal interviews with the providers you like the best.

Before beginning the process of searching for childcare, look at a map. Highlight the areas of town which are convenient for pick-up and drop off. If one parent is going to be primarily responsible for picking up and dropping off, you may want to choose childcare between their work and home. If one parent will be picking up and the other dropping off, choose childcare as close to home as possible, or closest to the parent who is first to be contacted in an emergency.

There are a million questions to ask a provider. It is important to prioritize what is crucial to your family when it comes to daycare. If your child has a cat allergy, the first question you should ask is "Do you have cats?" Cross every provider who does from your list. We of course recommend crossing off anyone who lives in a home where there is smoking. Providers will make the excuse that they smoke outside, but they are cuddling your child against their fog covered clothes. If there is a dog in the home, ask if the dog is allowed to play with the daycare children. If the answer is yes, be careful. It is a huge risk to expose even the gentlest of dogs to a ton of people every day, especially the type of people who will stick things up the dog's nose or climb all over him. If the dog is kept separate from the children it should be a non-issue except with a child who has an allergy. Once again, a provider will swear their dog wouldn't harm a fly. No dog comes with a guarantee. It also isn't fair to the dog.

Begin your weeding out process by starting with providers who are registered or licensed in your state. Although having a license is not a guarantee of quality, it does mean someone is occasionally checking up on that provider. Try to find providers who are on the food program, which ensures your child is well fed. We explain registration and the food program in a later chapter.

When calling providers, try to be considerate of what they do for a living. Try to avoid early morning when parents are dropping off, lunch time and afternoons from 4:30 to 6:00 PM. Most providers will say that the best time to call is from 1-3 PM or after 6. Always ask the provider if this is a good time. If it isn't, don't be offended if they ask you to leave your number.

The next two pages are a checklist of questions to ask a provider. You can use these as a guideline for interviewing on the phone or in person. You may find you can make a decision about someone with the answers to just one or two questions, but there are some you need to ask anyone you are considering.

NOTE: It is rude to make your first questions to a provider about cost. If you want a great relationship with your provider, your first concern should be her qualifications and experience, not how cheap her rates are. Although cost is an important consideration, childcare is too important to base solely on the money. Find a provider you love, and give up the extras you have to in order to afford her.

The following checklist may not have every question you need answered. It will help you to get started.

Childcare Interview Checklist: **Crucial yet overlooked questions are in bold.**

1. Are you licensed/registered? If so, what level of registration do you have?
2. How many providers are in your home/center?
3. **How many children are you currently caring for?**
4. What is the age range of children you watch?
5. I will need childcare from _____ to _____. Are those hours within your business hours?
6. Tell me about your experience with children. Do you have children? How long have you done childcare?
7. What is the daily schedule like in your childcare?
8. **Will you be transporting my child in a vehicle? If so, where will you go and how often? Does your vehicle insurance cover daycare transportation?**
9. **Are you currently certified in CPR and 1st Aid?**
10. Does your childcare participate in the food program?
11. What type of education do you have? Do you take continuing education courses to stay current in childcare issues?
12. What are your policies on illness? Vacation? Personal days?
13. What holidays are you closed?
14. Do you have an emergency plan in place and perform drills for fire, tornado . . . ?
15. **If there is an emergency, where will my child be taken?**
16. **Has everyone in your household had a physical and background check?**
17. **Has anyone in your household been convicted of a crime, including sex offenses, D.U.I.'s, suspended driver's licenses or other misdemeanors or felonies?** (This information can be verified through public records and the State Licensing agency)
18. **Has your license to practice childcare ever been suspended or revoked, even temporarily?** (You can verify this info.)
19. **What are your feelings about discipline? How will my child be disciplined for the following..**
    Biting   Hitting   Not sharing Lying
20. What type of activities do you offer for my child? Are there preschool activities provided for my child when they become preschool age?

21. **Do you carry childcare insurance? Are parents able to view a copy of the policy?**
22. What types of pets live in your household? Are they around the children regularly?
23. **Do you have current vaccinations and health checks for all the animals in your home?**
24. What meals and snacks do you provide?
25. What supplies will I need to provide for my child?
26. If I have questions or concerns, how should I address them with you?
27. If you have concerns about my child, how will you let me know?
28. Do you meet with parents regularly?
29. **Do you have access to testing materials to make sure my child is on track?**
30. What are some important things you like for new parents to know about your childcare?
31. If I choose to breast feed, can you accommodate me? Can I come here on my lunch to nurse my child?
32. **Will my child have her own bed for sleeping? If not, can I provide one and will you keep other children out of it?**
33. **When was your last daycare inspection and what, if anything, were you required to change?** (This info can be verified with the State Licensing agency)

There are bound to be more questions you will have for providers. The last thing you should ask is about what they charge. If you are seeking part-time childcare, understand that it is more expensive than full time. Don't be afraid to pay for a full-time slot with a provider you like, as long as you let her know that you will expect to use some of the extra time for doctor's visits, grocery shopping etc . . . . ANOTHER NOTE: Just because you pay by the week does not mean you should max out your time every week. You are cheating your child if you are not working but still leave them in childcare. It is always considerate to pick your child up early or keep them home when you can. Even though your childcare provider may have other children regardless, one less makes for an easier day. Your provider will appreciate your concern for your child and for their mental health. Don't make excuses about keeping your child on a schedule. You should have your child on the same schedule at home that they are at childcare anyway, so there should be no problem with you keeping your own child when you are not at work. The purpose of daycare is to provide an alternative to your care when you can't be available. It is not intended to be a dumping ground so that you can have time to relax. Once you have a child, being there to raise them needs to be your first priority. Your provider may assure you it is no big deal. To your child it is.

When sitting with a provider for an interview, it is just as important to look around at your surroundings and observe the provider with your child, her children and her daycare children if they are present. Does she express interest in your child? Does she talk to your child or hold them while she talks with you? Does she inquire about their schedule, their health and your expectations for them? Any provider should show an interest in finding out about your child. After all, she is making a commitment to watch a child she knows nothing about. Pay attention to how she deals with her own children. Do they seem to mind and respect her? Do they seem out of control and aggressive? Remember they will also be around your child all day. In addition, if the provider you are interviewing is harsh or inappropriate with her own children, do not assume she will be any nicer to your child. Thank her for her time and move on.

It is crucial to pay attention to safety and sanitary aspects of a childcare home. Pay close attention to the following:

1. Are there poisons down where a child could reach them? Medicines on the counter, bug spray or cleaners on the table, or other poisonous items your child could ingest. If your child is an infant, these things still matter because before you know it your child will be climbing up to those counters. If another child should happen to be poisoned while your child is there it could cause terrible consequences for you and your child.
2. There is a difference between clutter and dirty. Toys and blankets lying all over are one thing, baseboards with food all over them is another thing altogether.
3. There is no harm in using the bathroom. Bathrooms that the toilets are disgusting and the sinks are grimy are an indication of

less than regular cleaning. Even worse, she may have cleaned up before you arrived and this may be her idea of spic and span.
4. Check the condition of the toys. Are they dirty, broken or inappropriate for your child? If you have an infant and there are tiny Lego's or army men lying around, think twice.

While you are talking to the provider, listen carefully to what she says about her other parents and the children in her care. Is she negative about them or does she seem to really like them? Is she full of complaints about her job or does she appear to thrive on caring for children? If she tells you their personal information, she will probably disclose yours. You should immediately leave if it begins to become apparent that her life is full of drama and mess, such as children in juvenile detention or lawsuits against parents.

Before you even go to an interview, ask the provider if she is willing to agree to a background check. There are companies on the internet that will help you check out the background of any prospective provider. Most states have their court records on-line so that you can see if the provider has been sued by parents or are in the habit of suing parents. The Dept. of Human Services will have background checks on file, but in most states they only check for child abuse. I recommend you do a little research on your own. In the back of this book, along with the listings of licensing agencies for each state we have included information for companies to use, on-line court records for the states that have them and more.

Never hire a childcare provider or center without references. Ask for a minimum of three and take the time to call them. Ask them what they like best, what they would change and how long they have been with the provider. If a provider has been doing childcare for several years and all her references have been with her for 2 months, there might be some turnover there.

One of the most common questions parents ask is whether to use a center or a home provider. There are absolutely pros and cons to both. Here is a list showing some of the great and not so great things about each type of facility.

Home Provider versus Center

Center Pros:

1. Because of the facility license, a center is required to be inspected more often and more in-depth than home childcares.
2. There are several adults in a center, which theoretically means they are monitoring each other.
3. Some centers offer great preschool programs
4. Children are in a room with other children their own age

Center cons:

1. Because your child is exposed to 15 children instead of 6, they are more often exposed to illness.
2. Centers rely on staff to do the cleaning every day. Since they do not live there, center staff may not clean as thoroughly as they would probably clean the home where their child plays also.
3. Class sizes are larger in centers because of State regulations. Therefore your child may receive less one on one attention.
4. Centers are less flexible when it comes to hours. They do not have the ability to keep your child in case of an emergency like a home provider would.
5. Staff members in childcare centers make an average of $8.00 per hour. As a result, this attracts young, inexperienced individuals who often do not have children of their own. In addition, the staff turnover in centers is tremendous. Your child may change caregivers multiple times per year, which is detrimental to their emotional security. Finding a childcare center where the staff is provided free childcare is the most desirable. You will find these centers have much better staff that stays much longer. Ask how long their employees have been there and what benefits they offer in order to keep turnover low.
6. You cannot have the in-depth interview with each teacher in a center that you can have with a home provider. And you have no choice when your child changes teachers because of staff changes. Make sure you ask how employees are checked. If all they do is the bare minimum State required child abuse check—be advised

that this is not adequate used alone. See if they do a complete background check of their own, if they drug test, and if they check all references.
7. Because training records are the responsibility of the center, every time a worker goes to a new center, the clock starts over on training. This means that a caregiver can go from center to center and never have to actually have CPR, 1st Aid and Universal Precautions. Since centers loathe spending money on training until they know an employee is going to be a safe bet, this happens far more often that parents realize. Make sure if you choose a center that they require both in-house and DHS training, and ask if training records are available for parents to view.

Home Providers:

Pros:

1. Your child will build a long term bond with one, maybe two caregivers and will stay with those same individuals long term. Home providers traditionally keep clients much longer, so your child will make long term bonds with other children in the daycare, as well as the provider's children. Even if your provider changes helpers, she will still be a long term figure in your child's life. There are centers that are owner run and these are the best option if you choose the center route.
2. In order to keep their own child from becoming ill, a home provider will sometimes be more vigilant about separating and sending home children who are ill. In addition, numbers don't lie. If your child is in a home with 8 children, statistics show they will be exposed to less illness than in a center with 30.
3. Home Providers have the ability to be more flexible in a lot of areas, such as arrival and departure times, items that can be brought to daycare, toilet training and more.
4. The percentage of home providers who quit childcare within the first five years is much lower than the percentage of childcare center staff who quit within two. That alone is a reason to stick with home care.

5. Home providers are available for communication far more readily than center staff. You cannot simply call your child's teacher in a center. You have to speak with a director, who then has to talk with the teacher, and someone will get back to you. With a home childcare, you call the person who is caring for your child directly.
6. In a home childcare, if another child becomes ill, because of the close knit relationship you will know sooner and have more information about what is wrong, and therefore what to watch your child for.
7. As your child grows, they will spend almost 20 years in some type of institutional school environment. By placing them in a home setting, you are providing them with a more family oriented setting, and avoiding the institution for a few more years.
8. Because of the lower overhead, the cost of a home provider is much more reasonable for a parent. I know, we said don't ask about cost, didn't we? After all the other factors it will come into play, and there is a difference of sometimes $100 per week or more per child.

Everything we considered ended up coming out on the side of the home provider. Although centers are a perfectly good solution, there really is no better person to raise your child than someone who will make them feel like they are at a second home all day. Find someone who will be around for years and form a lasting bond with your child and your family.

Once you have chosen the perfect Mary Poppins for your little tyke, it is crucial that you start off on the right foot and stay there. The next chapter is all about daycare parent etiquette and strong communication.

The next chapter is intended to educate you about things that may offend your provider or weaken the trust between the two of you. The story below from a provider may help you to understand why it is so important.

I have always told my parents that if they are not going to be at work, they need to pick up their child. I make exceptions if they are doing something

Theresa J. Mulhern

their child cannot be a part of, such as painting the kitchen or going to couple's therapy. But it has always been my stance that if you are not working, your child needs time with you. I always thought they knew that they should let me know if they weren't going to be at work because it is clearly outlined in my handbook.

So imagine if you will, the Jones's 3 year old falling down on my deck and landing on the toy she had been playing with right on her teeth. She couldn't have hit that metal truck more perfectly if she tried, and I was looking at the first injury in 10 years that was going to need more than a Band-Aid and a kiss.

I called in my neighbor to help my assistant with the other children. I prepared for the trip to the emergency room. Because of field trips and transportation, I keep updated emergency contact and medical authorization sheets in my car. I loaded up Anna and took off with my cell phone in hand. At the first stop light I dialed the first number, which was dad's work. I asked politely for Mark Jones. The woman on the other end sounded tense. "Can anyone else help you?" she asked. I politely told her no, that I was his childcare provider and that his child had been injured so if she could please page him I would be grateful. Imagine my shock when the voice on other end informed me Anna's dad had left their employment more than a month before! I hung up before I could ask if they knew where I could find him. I went to the next number on his list, his cell phone. I wasn't really shocked to find it was disconnected . . . His job was for a cell phone company and I imagined the phone was one of his perks.

Next on the list was Mom's work. By now I was pulling into the hospital parking lot and getting worried. Although I had more than enough of the necessary paperwork, I don't like making decisions about medical care for a child that isn't mine. And now I didn't even know how to list dad's information or even if their insurance was any good.

I got voice mail at mom's work. I left a brief message that she needed to call my cell phone as soon as possible and looked for another contact number. Mom's cell was a bust just like dads. I checked into the emergency room, authorized Anna's cut super glued shut (personally guaranteeing payment because of course the insurance was no-longer any good), signed the bill and left with a prescription and a case of the ass.

I was halfway done with the 20 minute drive home (after the 2 hours in the ER) when mom called with a casual "What's up?"

"I am pretty sure that's the question I should be asking you." I said as calmly as I could. "We had a tumble this morning and your daughter ended up needing to see a doctor. She's fine now but she does have a cut that required gluing." I took a deep breath, unsure whether to light into her or cut her a little slack while she recovered from the news her child had gotten hurt. I then started the crucial conversation. "Amy, were you ever going to tell me your husband left his job? And do you have new contact information you can give me tonight because I need to be able to reach you in cases like this. I should not be the one authorizing medical treatment for your child when you are 10 minutes from the hospital and I'm 20."

There was silence on the other end of the phone. I wasn't surprised. Here was mom, who knew my policy on parents keeping their child when not at work, trying to figure out a plausible explanation why her child had been coming to daycare 11 hours a day while dad was at home not working. It was a full 4 seconds before the excuses began.

"I thought I told you Mark got fired the beginning of last month. We didn't want to disrupt Anna's schedule. Besides, his job right now is looking for a job." She paused for a moment and then made the comment that sent me through the roof. "It's actually been great with him being home all day. He's getting the yard work all done and a ton of stuff around the house fixed. He's even been making dinner for us before he leaves to wait tables at Jimmy's, which is making him enough to hold us over for a while."

Right about this time I was getting off the Interstate. I have never been one who can drive and digest information at the same time. So I told mom I would need to hang up to deal with traffic and got off the phone to deal with my anger. I thought about how great it would be to have time to do my own yard work, or make my family dinner at a decent time instead of ordering take-out after getting the last kid out the door. I thought about Anna, who had been so whiny for the last couple of weeks that I was sure she was turning psychotic. It would have been so nice to know about the upheaval at home, or about the fact she wasn't even seeing her father anymore because he left for the Cafe before she got home. I thought about how badly this could have gone if her injuries had been severe. The more I thought the madder I got.

It got worse. The next week dad got a new job that didn't start for 2 weeks. I assumed this would mean that since he had found a job, his job wasn't finding a job anymore. How many days did he keep his child to spend time with her before starting the new job? You guessed it—Zippo! I gave notice the moment I secured a new family to replace the income. Now they're really disrupting Anna's schedule!

There is a very fine line between using and abusing daycare. Here's my thought. If you are not at work, your number one job is to parent your own child. If you want your child to behave for you in public, don't leave them at the sitter's house while you grocery shop and run errands. Take them with you to see your new friend's baby and to pick out your book at Barnes and Noble. Your daycare provider manages to take her child with her everywhere, because she doesn't have a daycare provider of her own. She even has to take your child occasionally. If she can do it, you can too. Remind yourself that time with your child is precious, even when it isn't relaxing quiet time at home.

Now let's talk about ways to build a trusting relationship with your provider.

Your Expectations of Childcare

One warning I always give any parent who is looking for childcare is that it is crucial not to have unrealistic expectations. Even though you want the very best care for your child, you have to understand that the very best care would be you staying home. Next best would be your child spending the day with grandma or Aunt Suzie who never was able to have kids of her own. If you are going to place your child in any form of childcare, including a nanny in your home, that person is a substitute and will never do things the same way you would.

That said—the biggest reason parents go from provider to provider is that no-one makes them happy when it comes to caring for their child. There are a lot of things that make parents want to leave a daycare. They may feel their child is not being held enough. Or it might be that when their child cries the response from the daycare provider isn't immediate. Maybe they feel their child is trapped in a pac-n-play a little too often.

The stress of one bad day can cause a fracture that can't be repaired. Try this one on for size:

About the time I was pregnant with my 8th child I got a new family with a little boy named Samuel. Samuel was adorable, with big eyes and an infectious smile. He was also the most curious child on the face of the earth. Samuel loved to pull outlet covers out of outlets, and sneak up the stairs whenever the gate wasn't up. He would bang on the front of the new big screen TV with the wooden spoon in the kitchen cabinet he rifled through. On most days it was amusing to watch. Some days it was more than 3 adults could take.

Theresa J. Mulhern

When I interviewed with Samuel's parents it was clear to me that mom wanted to stay home, and that no daycare was going to be good enough. She eagle-eyed my entire house and wanted to know how many minutes at a time her child would be in any kind of restraint. Her theory was that if he was put in a saucer or pac-n-play for more than 50 nanoseconds, his brain would turn to mush and he would be behind developmentally. This was something she just could not have!

I was completely shocked when they hired me a day later and came and paid their deposit. By the time Samuel started I had received 5 emails from mom with instructions for his first day. The first week they made surprise visits every day to check and make sure that their child wasn't tied to the chair. The second week there were announced visits because they were going to be in the area (not). Things settled into a nice rhythm until the day I placed Samuel in a swing to change some babies with dirty diapers. Low and behold mom showed up early and the Shit hit the fan.

I knew from the look on her face that mom was struggling not to say anything. She took Samuel and went out the door. I watched casually as she got in her car and immediately began talking on her cell phone to someone I assume must have been her husband. Twenty minutes later there was an email in my inbox from dad's work. It read . . . .

>Terri,
>
>My wife and I are concerned that Samuel is spending too much time in confined equipment such as infant seats, baby swings, play pens, and exer-saucers. It is difficult to view these devices in a positive light as they are little more than cages or the equivalent of tying a child to a chair. At home we have gates preventing access to the stairs and child safety locks on cabinet doors and drawers. These precautions ensure his safety and allow him to move freely around large play areas. It is important to us that, at his stage of development, he is able to walk and crawl distances greater than 5 or 6 steps. Therefore, we never put him in any type of confining equipment at home with the exception of a high chair for meals and snacks and a crib when he sleeps.

It is understandable to put him in a seat that he cannot move around in when he is eating. Although we would prefer he ate his meals in a high chair, I respect the convenience an infant seat affords. The important thing is he is not allowed to run around with food or drink. An infant seat is adequate for that purpose. It is also acceptable that he sleeps in a pack and play when necessary until you move to your new location. We expect that he will only sleep in a crib at the new location until he is old enough to sleep on a floor mat. Please inform us if this is not the case.

I do not understand why he would be in any type of restraining equipment outside of meals, snacks, or sleep time. I would not want to be tied down to a chair or confined in a closed space for any period of time and cannot imagine he would want to be either. If there are too many children to keep track of or you are unable to prevent personal injury without putting him in restraints it is important to us that we know this. That way we can make educated decisions about the level of care he is receiving and determine whether or not it is acceptable.

I would like to discuss this further when I drop Samuel off in the morning. Thank you for your attention to this matter.

Thanks,
Mike

I read the email and tried to decide how to respond. Do I tell them that their child spends 99% of his time running around the house and that 1% of the time in a pac-n-play won't kill him? Do I lie and tell them it will never happen again? The fact of the matter was that I couldn't promise that. I had placed their child in a swing while changing a dirty diaper, because it was impossible to chase him and clean up a poopy child. I had set his child in a saucer while serving the bigger kids lunch, while waiting for his lunch to be ready. I had placed his child in a play-yard during pick-up time to keep him from walking out the door that parents tend to leave wide open, because they are too busy chasing their own child to look out for the rest by shutting the door. I decided I would be tactful but truthful. Here was my response.

> Michael:
>
> I had Samuel in the swing for about 4 minutes today while I was changing 2 other poopy diapers because he kept heading for the kitchen and the gate was not up at the top of the stairs. I would not want him to try to go down to the playroom and fall down the stairs.
>
> Samuel is in a playpen/ crib for naptime only. He is allowed to run free for 6 hours during the day in the playroom which is childproofed every night. The main floor of the house right now is not childproof because of the move. I understand you want Samuel to be free but I know you also want him to be safe. He was not unhappy or upset in the swing and had only been there for a few minutes when mom came. He is in a highchair or the rocker/saucer when he has snack. If you prefer the highchair to the rocker it is fine.
>
> I know mom is nervous about Samuel. I am a mom and can appreciate your concerns, and I will make sure your child has all the freedom he needs to stay on track with motor development. Please be understanding that beginning and end of day there will be occasional times he won't be able to wander the main floor and will have to stay in the living room with us. And every now and then he will need to be restrained for his own safety.
>
> Terri

I felt I had responded honestly and waited to hear. There was no mention of any of it by dad after that. 2 weeks later we moved and before I had even gotten unpacked mom came with her notice in hand. She expressed that she wanted to stay home, and that they were not leaving because they were unhappy with me. She cried and seemed very sincere. I don't know if she meant it and I will always wonder if every day they had visions of their child starving to death trapped in a dungeon in a dark room. After they left, they went back to a center. It wasn't long before the center was in the hot seat, because a teacher had placed him in a crib for an hour in an effort to stop him from bullying other children. Unfortunately the center forgot that there were cameras attached to the internet and what they didn't know was that mom dressed Samuel in bright orange jumpsuits so she could watch the monitors constantly and make sure her little sweetie wasn't being neglected. This error in judgment resulted in hours of meetings with the director and the teacher, in order to ensure they would never screw up again.

Let's face it: some parents just will never be satisfied with the way someone else will raise their child. I wish them the best. In 25 years I have been fired 6 times. All 6 times were parents who I knew from day one would probably never hire me and definitely wouldn't last.

There are so many ways a provider can fall short of your expectations. We are, after all human. We are parents who during the day are raising a half a dozen or more children. Imagine you had a half a dozen children under the age of 4. Could you hold one child all the time? Could you run right away when a child who has just been fed and changed begins fussing? Probably not. Here are some sticking points that seem to cause problems a lot and how to work them out.

You should expect your provider to hold your child. You should not expect her to hold your child all day, even if he cries like mad every time she puts him down. As my mother used to say to me when I had my first, "No child ever died from crying". Although the statement is true, it can be excruciating for a new mom to hear her baby cry for even a minute.

So here's the scoop. You will probably arrive a lot of times to find your child in a saucer or bouncy seat, because during pick up time we providers have to deal with finding shoes and socks, talking with parents and kissing little ones goodbye. If your child seems content sitting there you can be assured he is getting the holding he needs. If on the other hand he is crying uncontrollably every day when you pick him up you may have cause to be concerned. Before you go looking for new daycare, drop in for a couple of unannounced visits an hour or so early. Be prepared to take your child with you rather than leaving him upset after seeing you. If when you show up unannounced your child is always in his swing screaming, it is time to discuss the issue with your provider.

Don't assume that because your child fusses to be held every night that he is not getting held during the day. Children know your smell and will want time with you when you are away all day. In addition children as young as 6 weeks will learn the new mommy equation which is C=PMU (crying = pick me up)! My equation for success is this: 75% autonomy and 25% TLC. You should not be holding your child, even a tiny infant, more than half of their waking moments. Try holding your child for 15 minutes, then putting them down for 15. Slowly increase this until you are holding your child no more than one fourth of the time. One fourth of the time is fine as long as your child is content playing with his toes or rolling around on the floor. If your child begins crying the moment you put them down, check the obvious first. Check their diaper, do a mental inventory of when they ate last and if they finished eating. Then try the Faucet test. Here's how . . . .

Walk over and lean over your child. If he immediately stops crying and smiles at you he is practicing playing you like a violin. Don't you dare get played! If you pick him up and he begins laughing, put him back down and see if he has a nuclear meltdown. If so, you will have to let Chernobyl implode or you will be chained to a child who screams day and night because he can't calm himself. In other words, if they shut off like a faucet the moment you give in, you have failed the test. It's not just your sanity at stake. Children need time on their own to learn to self-comfort and play. They have to be put down in order to learn important skills such as rolling over and crawling. If you feel your provider is holding your child too much, let her know that you want your child to have more time on his own on the floor to develop his skills. Your provider knows this, and chances are she has her own equation that works great.

The next area that gets parents crazy is the diapers. Your child should not be coming home every week with a diaper rash. There will be times, however, that you will pick him up and he will be wet or soiled. Just like there will be times you will put a clean diaper on him to go out to dinner and he will reek by the time you are sitting down at Red Lobster (they love that there, I know from experience).

If you are putting a clean diaper on your child every morning before you leave for daycare, you should expect your provider to go through a minimum of 1 diaper for every two to three hours your child is in care. If you are not putting a clean diaper on your child before leaving for daycare you need to let your provider know so that your child's diaper doesn't end up leaking all over her couch because she expected your child to be clean and dry when arriving (and she has a right to have this expectation). If you are supplying diapers it is easy enough to make sure this minimum is being met. Bear in mind that this is a minimum, because generally a good provider will check diapers every 2 hours. If your child develops a diaper rash during the week that goes away on the weekend and comes back by Tuesday, do not wait to talk to your provider. Supply her with the ointment you would like used and let her know that your child needs more frequent changing. If your child develops rashes on the weekends as well, it is probably an allergy to the perfumes and dyes in the diaper, acidic urine caused by too much juice or tomato products or maybe a yeast infection. Talk with your pediatrician to try to pinpoint the problem. Here's a good rule of thumb. Unless your child is on antibiotics frequently, which can cause diaper rashes from yeast, your child should not be having more than 4-6 diaper rashes per year, and they should clear up easily with cream and frequent changing.

You also need to be prepared to step up your game if your child has a diaper rash on the weekends that clears up every week and then comes back when your child is home with you. If that is the case, you need to make sure you are checking your child's diaper often. If they develop a bad rash, get a bottle like the ones that you use in restaurants to fill with ketchup. Each time you change your child, wipe the ointment off with a wipe that is alcohol free. Then use the bottle to squirt warm water with baby wash in it to wash your child's bottom thoroughly. You can put a towel under their butt to soak up the water. Let their bottom dry thoroughly before putting any kind of ointment on, because otherwise you are sealing in moisture which can lead to yeast infections. Repeat this process every diaper change until your child's bottom is absolutely clear. In the last chapter of the book there is a recipe for a diaper rash compound that you can use to kill the worst of rashes.

Next expectation that never gets met: the belief that other children will always be sweet to your child. Whenever several children are placed in one space together, there will be the one child who is going through a hitting or biting phase. There will be the child who likes babies but hasn't learned how to be gentle. There will also be the days when your child is that one child.

Absolutely your child has a right to be safe in daycare. You should not be seeing black eyes and fat lips from Johnny B every week. Your child should not be coming home with bite marks every other day. If your child is being attacked by the one child, don't panic. Ask your provider about separating the two children as much as possible. When it is your child being the one, don't make excuses. Talk with your child about nice friends and kindness and don't ask what the other child was doing that made it acceptable for your child to bite a chunk out of him, because you know better.

If you have a good childcare provider, you can expect they will be teaching your child. If you are expecting your child to come home every day at the age of 2 with a craft project or worksheet you are among the parents who are guilty of another unrealistic expectation. This is the expectation that your child isn't being taught unless there is a lot of tangible crap coming home every night to clutter up your counters.

The truth is that even in Kindergarten a majority of what kids learn every day does not require paper or pen and doesn't generate anything cute to look at. Your child will be learning how to get along, how to play dress-up and how to pick up their own toys. They will learn how to feel empathy and dozens of new words to use. These things are important and although you can't see proof, if you ask your child about their day you can evaluate what each activity would be good for. If they played restaurant, they are learning communication and creative play. If they had music time they are learning songs practicing rhythm and rhyme. Treasure the craft projects and pictures they bring home and remember it is quality, not quantity that counts.

The one expectation that makes us providers the craziest are parents who expect we will deny their children a much needed nap so that they can get them into bed at night with no argument. Children need a rest during the day up until age 6. They may not need to fall asleep, but they do need to lie down and rest. In addition, daycare is not like a corporate job. From the time the first child arrives in the morning until the last child leaves at night, providers do not have the luxury of a lunch or smoke break. We are literally with our clients all day long without any reprieve. Imagine your crankiest client and imagine spending the entire day with him in your face without a moment to yourself. Naptime is the one time of day that your provider can clean up all the mess, eat her own cold lunch and do all the paperwork necessary to keep her license current. You can negotiate with your provider the length of your child's rest within reason, but be mindful of the fact that if your provider can get your child to fall asleep every day with no problem, and you are struggling to get them to bed on the weekends when they are with you, it may be an issue of parental control at bedtime and not an issue of too much nap.

There are at least a hundred things that parents expect that daycare providers could never provide. My contract has a paragraph that sums it up . . . .

We want to know if you have concerns. Before you start looking around for new daycare, we hope you will come and talk to us. It does not have to be confrontational; it can simply be that things are worrying you. I am a parent, and I do understand the fears of leaving your child somewhere while you work. I will tell you honestly if I can help fix what is wrong. I will also tell you if I feel you have unrealistic expectations. A simple rule of thumb is as follows: Do not expect me to do more while caring for your child than you do. If you don't read to your child 2 hours a day please don't expect us to. We are here to give your child a loving environment that is safe. You have the right to expect your child will be well fed, have safe toys to play with, and to receive good supervision and nurturing care. We cannot feed your child whatever he wants to eat, as much as we would like to. We cannot allow your child to sit on our lap all day; he needs to learn to play with others. We will not allow your child to be unkind or disrespectful, because that would be a disservice to him and to you. We will hug and hold your child frequently. We will give him fruits and vegetables, milk and meat and 100% juice. We will lay him down for a rest (until age 6) even though we cannot promise he will sleep. We will teach love, respect and the alphabet whenever possible. So please, ask for what you would like and then listen to what we say as well.

Sounds reasonable . . . . Doesn't it?

When Standard Options Cannot Meet Your Needs

Under certain circumstances parents may have to choose one type of childcare over another. While no one type of childcare is right for every family, you can decide ahead of time the best type of childcare to fit your situation. Here are some special circumstances that need special types of care.

If you have a child with an illness such as Spina-Bifida or Cerebral-Palsey, you obviously have to be very selective about where you leave your child. The best two options for a child with medical needs are a special needs facility or a nanny in your own home. Before hiring a nanny you will either need to find one who already has the medical training that is relevant to your child or be willing to pay to have her trained before she starts. Don't be afraid to take suggestions from other parents in a support group, they may know of a great nanny who is looking for a family. Unfortunately, nannies that care for ill children are sometimes left without a job because a child who was terminally ill has passed away.

Find out from your doctor where a support group is for your child's illness. In addition, find out where your nanny can receive training in skills she will need, such as handling colostomy bags or cleaning tracheotomy tubes. If you can afford to do so, send her to a Certified Nurse's Aide class nights or weekends, with the condition that if she stays with you less than 1 year the cost of the class will be deducted from her final check. Your local hospital will have specialists and classes available for anyone who needs to learn how to care for an ill child. Go with your nanny to these classes if you can and make sure she is attentive and is catching on to the skills. You should pay attention too, as these are skills you will need at night and on the weekend.

If you decide to go with a facility, check them out. Contact the state and ask about their inspections and if there are complaints that were founded. Ask about the training their staff receives and ask how often they are inspected. Make a play date and watch how things are done in the room you will have your child in. Watch to see how often they are changing the children and dealing with things such as colostomy treatment and catheters and take note if they do it often enough to avoid infection or complications. See if they interact with the children or just house them. It is especially important to pay attention to the health and sanitary practices of the staff. Children with chronic illness are more susceptible to bacteria, so the hand washing has to be done and the sanitizing of changing tables and toys is crucial in order to keep your child from contracting an infection or illness.

If you are going to consider in-home childcare for a special needs child because of the cost or other factors, place your child in a home daycare with no more than 4 children total, including the provider's. In addition make sure they don't have more than 2 children with special needs total. The provider may assure you she has time to care for your special needs child along with 6 others, but the fact is that she's either crazy or really needs a bigger paycheck. Both are reasons to walk away. Ask any in-home provider you interview to provide copies of training showing they are capable of dealing with your child's condition.

Another reason for not using conventional centers or in-home childcare is an unusual schedule. Most women who choose to do in-home childcare work the hours that their husbands work in order to spend time with their family evenings and weekends. This means that if you work nights and weekends, you may not be able to find a center or in-home daycare that is open the hours you work. Your options are to hire a nanny or have someone in your family/friend support system watch your child. Start by asking around if any of your friends would be interested in watching your child for you. Make it clear that you are offering to pay and offer a rate that is fair for the hours you are asking for. If you choose to hire a nanny, make it clear to every applicant the hours you work, so that they don't think the interview is for a daytime job. If you are hiring a nanny for unusual hours, go the live-in route if at all possible. That way there are no sick call-ins on a Friday night 10 minutes before you have to go to work.

If you are a parent who likes to keep their children very occupied, a nanny is really the only sensible solution. A center or provider can't take your child to a new set of lessons each week. If you want scouts, karate and gymnastics and you don't want to be doing the hauling, find yourself a great nanny who will happily sit and do her college homework while your child karate chops other 6 year olds. The same applies if you are a very active parent with lots of social engagements. You will want continuity of care for your child. It is crazy to take a child from daycare during the day and plant them with a night sitter at night.

If you are a parent whose job takes you out of town overnight or for days at a time, there are two ways you can handle it. You can have a friend or family member who picks your child up from daycare and takes them home, or you can hire a live-in nanny and pay her with comp-time or extra pay when you have to be gone. Once again be very clear when hiring this individual that this is part of the job.

Believe it or not, there are some children that are simply not social creatures. They don't want to be in a room full of children. In some cases it can be extreme and cause a child anxiety, even to the point of ulcers. If your child is one of these rare children and you can afford it, hire someone in house. Trying to make your child be social will only make them neurotic and agoraphobic. You can gradually work them in to the social frame of mind by taking them places and staying there while they get adjusted.

There are other circumstances where daycare centers or registered daycare homes may not work for a family. Although centers and RH's try to accommodate all religious needs, if you pray every two hours and eat a halal diet, a friend or family member who understands the importance of your practices is the best choice. Even someone with the best of intentions might not remember everything all the time. Here is a great example:

> Harry is the most adorable 18 month old god ever made. He also has a severe allergy to nuts. Thank god we didn't find that out at my house. Anyway, mom had tried giving him peanut butter and it resulted in a trip to the hospital and an overnight stay. As I had

never had a child with a nut allergy, I had no idea how many products have nuts or nut oils in them I also had no idea how severe nut allergies were.

I had gone through my cabinets and eliminated all things nutty. I had made a menu that only served peanut butter on days when Harry was at home with mom. I had posted allergy reminders everywhere for my helpers and I to remind us of the situation. I forgot to educate mom on how to do these things at home.

The phone call came at 8 AM.

"Harry won't be there today. I have to give my two week notice and he won't be there for that either"

"What's the matter Heidi?" I asked. There had been no indication she was anything less than thrilled with us as providers.

"I can't do this anymore" Now she was sobbing. "I can't trust anyone to watch him and I leave for one minute and end up with a hospital bill. I quit my job today and they are so angry. I just want one minute without freaking out!"

It turns out that she had left her brother watching her son the day before. Although her brother was very responsible, he had made a mistake without knowing it. He ate peanut butter M&Ms on the way to her house. While wrestling on the floor and hugging and kissing Harry, some of the peanut oil got on Harry's lips and bare skin. The result was another trip to the hospital, and another huge medical bill.

Although it may seem an extreme reaction for Heidi to pull her child from daycare where he had never been given nuts, I totally understood. You see, Heidi had been a stay at home mom until Harry was 11 months old. Then one morning her fiancé, Harry's dad, wrecked his motorcycle on his way to work and died. Because there was no will, Heidi had to move out of the house that was in his name. Being in their early 20's they had not thought about *things like life insurance, which meant that she had to go back to work and leave her child in daycare. I imagine the thought of losing her child less than a year after losing her husband made her panic. In the end it all worked out, because she began doing daycare to make ends meet and now is able to be with her child to meet his needs and still bring in a paycheck.*

Whatever your circumstances are, take a look at your options and be realistic about your needs. Don't plan to make changes that aren't practical. If you know you always work late, don't hire someone and promise them they'll be off at five o-clock. Give them the worst case scenario up front so that you know they are making an informed decision. Make sure your expectations are clear and in writing so that they understand. We cover contracts and job descriptions in a later chapter.

When Someone Else Pays the Bill

I loved watching the Jensen kids. Four very bright children they made my day full and exciting. Although they were on daycare assistance, I was OK with $125 per week per child because they were well behaved and left before 5 PM, which left me with fewer kids to handle while making dinner. It usually takes at least 2 months before getting paid for the first time for a state client, because you can only bill at the end of the month and it can take up to 45 days for the state to issue a check. I was so looking forward to spending the $3800 the State of Iowa owed me. Instead of a check however, I got a notice that their daycare bill would not be paid. As luck would have it, mom had not turned in her pay stubs showing a substantial raise. The result was that her assistance was cancelled back to the day she applied. So all of the money that I counted on to pay my staff and my property taxes which were due was gone. I was going to have to borrow against the hubby's 401K to even make it work. This was one of those days when I wanted to meet every parent at the door and tell them I was giving my 2-week's notice. It seemed no matter how hard I worked I ended up struggling more than I would just staying home and living off my husband's paycheck. The biggest disappointment was when mom announced since there was no way she could pay all the past due bill, she was simply going to move home to mom and send payments. Two years later and I haven't seen .10c, let alone $3800.00. I could sue her, but she doesn't have anything so I would simply be throwing good money after bad. Chalk it up to stupidity.

If you are a parent who qualifies for daycare assistance from the State or any other agency, you have a much more complicated road ahead when finding daycare. This can also be true if someone in your family or your employer is paying your childcare bill. Let's start with different kinds of public and private assistance and move on form there.

In the US, each state has its own program for daycare assistance. You can find the number for your state's program in the appendix of this book. Before finding daycare you will need to find out from the state what its requirements are. Some State assistance programs will pay for a provider who is not registered, such as your mom staying home with the grandkids. Some State programs only reimburse providers with a state contract. Almost every state requires that you choose a provider to put on your application. This means you should interview and select a provider and a back-up to put on the application for daycare, so that when one provider goes on vacation your back-up provider can bill the state with no issues or extra paperwork.

You will need to complete your application for assistance with all the relevant paperwork. Most states require you provide copies of your child's birth certificate as well as copies of your paystubs for the last 30 days and any court orders for child support you receive. It can take up to 45 days to get a decision back, so the sooner you apply the better. If you hire a provider before your baby is born, make sure they accept state assistance if you are planning on applying for it.

When you are using state assistance there are a few things you have to remember. First, your assistance will only pay for childcare for the things you are approved for. If your notice of decisions says that you are approved for work hours for 2 units a day, each unit is for up to five hours. However, if you only work seven hours you cannot run errands or have lunch with friends and expect your provider to bill the state. Providers are required to keep an accurate record of when your child arrives and leaves. Your assistance worker has the right to compare those hours with your work hours at any time to make sure that you and your provider are being honest.

Your notice of decision from the state will have requirements listed that you must comply with. These include sending in your paystubs at regular intervals, notifying the state if you move, change employment or have a change in circumstance such as getting married or getting a new job. Failure to comply with these will result in cancellation of your coverage, which means your provider will get a notice in the mail letting her know that your daycare bill is no longer being covered. It then can take weeks to get re-approved and in the meantime you will need to pay for childcare out of your pocket.

In addition, your provider will have a list of requirements she will need to fulfill. She will be keeping track of when your child is there and sending in monthly invoices. It is important you know what she is claiming for hours. There will be a form for you to sign verifying your child's hours. Do not sign blank forms for the state for your provider. If she claims more hours than your child was there and your signature is on that form, you will be in trouble and possibly lose your daycare assistance. She should have the forms all filled out before you sign them. If she is keeping records every day there should be no problem.

If you want to be really organized, each time you fill out a change form or application for the state, give a stamped copy of it to your provider for your child's file. This will help her to get paid faster if there is ever a problem with your approval.

Some individuals on daycare assistance have a co-pay. This is an amount that is your responsibility. It is crucial that you make sure this portion is paid on time and in-full. If you can arrange it, pay for your co-pay for 2-4 weeks at a time. It can take up to 3 months for your provider to get paid by the state for the first time, and your co-pay will help at least with feeding your child until the first state check arrives. But as state billing is done after the fact, it is an entire month before your provider can bill them for watching your child. It can then take up to 45 days to receive a check. In the back of this book you will find the listings for your state for childcare assistance.

The next type of childcare assistance is through Promise Jobs, or other unemployment agencies. This type of assistance is to help individuals who need temporary childcare assistance while going to school or job training, interviewing or working an apprenticeship or other short term employment related items.

The military also has childcare assistance, but theirs is very tricky. For example, in Iowa home providers are registered, not licensed. Same inspection and more training, but because they do not have the title *license* the military will not reimburse for in home childcare in Iowa. You can find the contact information about military daycare assistance in the back as well. The great thing about Military childcare assistance is that their income guidelines are much higher.

If your employer reimburses for childcare, inquire well before your baby is born how it works. If your child is due before the end of the tax year, ask about filling out the forms and having any pre-tax deductions in a flex plan come out now. That way when you find a provider and have to pay a deposit and the first week or month of care you will be ready to start getting money back in your check right away.

If you are relying on family or others for help with your childcare bill, let them know as far ahead as you can who you have chosen and if you are comfortable with doing so, include them in the decision. Make sure you are clear about the terms of their help and how long they will be helping for, so you can prepare for when the bill will revert back to you. Make sure if you are asking family for help that you have made every effort to help yourself, to include applying for childcare assistance with State and County agencies, so that they can see that you are making an honest effort not to put this bill off on them. Make a plan for getting yourself independent and make a plan for repaying the daycare help if you can, even if it is through cleaning their house or watching their children. And express to them constantly how much you appreciate the help, because it is a large expense for someone else to take on your behalf.

When you interview with your new provider, these items must be included in the discussion. Be prepared to pay a deposit for your childcare, even if you are on assistance. Most providers now charge a deposit to everyone, because parents who are on assistance often lose their assistance with no notice, and the provider is left with bills to pay and no income to cover them.

Check with your provider on a regular basis to make sure your assistance is getting paid. By asking how things are going you can find out right away if there is a problem and be proactive with your case worker or responsible party to get your provider paid.

If you are a parent whose estranged spouse is supposed to be paying your daycare bill, be prepared to pay if your ex does not come through. It is not your provider's fault if for any reason your ex decides not to hold up his end of the bargain, and she still deserves to be paid on time and in full. Use an advance on a credit card if you have to, but make sure your bill gets taken care of. The only thing worse for a child than divorce is divorce and then hopping from one daycare to another because daddy (or mommy) hasn't paid the bill. If at all possible have your ex pay you ahead of time or pay the provider by the month in order to lessen any issues that may come up.

If something goes wrong, don't panic. Be honest with your provider and tell them as soon as you know there is an issue. Offer to make payments to take care of your bill and do not be offended if your provider asks for a late fee. After all, the bills she will be paying late are going to charge her late fees for your lateness. It doesn't matter whose fault it is, it isn't your providers. Providers get taken every day by irresponsible people who run up a bill and then make excuses for not paying it. It is frustrating to be a provider who has a mortgage payment due and 2-3 parents who haven't paid their bill yet. It can make for some very sleepless nights for them, which doesn't leave them in the best frame of mind to be caring for your child. Remember that caring about your provider will make them more likely to care about you when you need something, such as extra time to work late or help with a problem with your child that is above and beyond their purview.

The bottom line with daycare is that it is a service you cannot live without. No matter who is responsible for paying, you still need to make sure that payment is getting to your provider in a timely fashion and step up to the plate when need be to make her feel secure about keeping your child. Nothing makes a provider give notice faster than having to fight to see a paycheck.

Before you apply for childcare assistance, get together everything you may need in a folder or envelope. The following items are things most state and local assistance agencies will want in order to process your application:

1. Proof of Identity: Place your driver's license, copy of your birth certificate and Social Security card in the envelope. These will also work for number 2 and number 3.

2. Proof of Citizenship
3. Tax Identification: Most state agencies get the money for daycare assistance from federal dollars. They have to keep your information and report it in order to receive these funds. Place everyone's social security cards in the envelope.
4. Proof of relation: If the children you want assistance for are your own, place their birth certificates in the envelope. If they are foster children, DHS will give you paperwork to use. If you are a guardian, place a copy of the court order in the envelope.
5. Proof of Income: Make sure you have your last 30 days of paystubs. If you are military use your last 4 LES's. If you receive child support, you must include this income and need a copy of the order for their records. The same is true of any other income, such as retirement, alimony and royalties or interest income. Foster and crisis care reimbursement is not considered income, and does not need to be listed. If you are self-employed you can provide your last year's income tax report.
6. Proof of what the assistance is for: If you are starting a new job, ask your employer for a letter on their letterhead. The letter needs to state when you will be starting, how many hours a week you will be working, what your schedule will be if it is set, and how much per hour you will be getting paid. If you are already working, you need a copy of your last schedule, and your paystubs will serve to prove your income and hours worked. If you are asking for assistance in order to use daycare while you look for a job you don't need paperwork for income. If you are applying for daycare assistance while you attend school, place a copy of your school schedule in the envelope.

It is important to understand how government childcare assistance works. You will apply and give them all of the necessary paperwork. It can take a while to get approved, so be proactive. When you receive your notice of decision it will tell you how many hours you get, what days of the week you can use those hours and what the hours are for. If you are approved for job search hours, you can only use them while you are actually applying or interviewing for jobs. School hours cannot be used for work and work hours cannot be used for grocery shopping. Your case worker can get copies of your work schedule at any time. It is simple for them to compare these with the attendance sheets that your provider has to turn in which tell when your child is dropped off and picked up every day. If you are using daycare hours that you are not working not only can they cancel your daycare assistance, they can bill you for any hours they paid for that you were not at work! So remember, don't abuse the privilege or you will lose it.

When you file your application, make a file in your personal records and file it away. Make sure you ask for copies that are stamped with the date received. Then take a copy to your provider so that she knows you are waiting for approval, and that she should plan on not receiving funds from you after you receive your approval. Ask your provider what happens if your approval is back-dated to the day you applied. Will she reimburse you for what has already been paid once you are approved, or will that money be applied to your co-pays until it is used up? If she is going to back bill and you have paid for the weeks pending approval, you are entitled to either a refund or a credit toward your co-pay (if you have one).

In order to make sure your approval stays in place, get out your planner when you get your notice of decision and mark the dates you have to turn in paperwork. Make sure you mark a reminder a few days ahead of time. For example, if your notice says that you have to turn in your next semester's school schedule by August 1st, mark a reminder to mail it on July 25th. If you have to turn in paystubs the end of September, write in your planner "Save Paystub for Assistance" on the 2 paydays preceding your due date so that you have them ready to go. Then make copies before you turn them in, just in case they get lost in the mail or in the pile on someone's desk. The best way to make sure your paperwork gets processed in a timely fashion is to turn it in personally, and get a stamped receipt.

Make sure you set aside a week's worth of daycare funds, even if you have to save $10 a week until you have it. Don't touch this money. Use it in an emergency when your daycare bill isn't paid for any reason and you need a cushion of time to fix the problem. Remember, it is just as important that your childcare provider have a check on payday as it is that you have one.

If you have a skill that your provider needs, never feel bad about asking if your provider might be willing to barter for part of your bill. I exchanged a $20 per week discount with one mom in return for her cutting my family's hair once a month. That may seem like a lot, but we have 8 kids and the 2 of us, so ten haircuts in our home without having to take 10 people to a salon is a great privilege.

Probably the best deal I ever made was with a mom who was a masseuse. She came to our home with her table every 2 weeks and gave my husband and I massages in return for $20 per week off her bill. And if any of my parents wanted massages they could get them twice a month at my house while she was there! We turned our spare room into a spa with music and candles and my daycare parents got a reduced rate from her. In the end not only did I help her get more business, eventually she didn't need help with her daycare bill anymore but still came to do massages for us.

If you are a contractor, plumber, electrician or any other skilled trade, make sure you let your provider know if you would be willing to do work for her and have your bill paid in childcare credit. I once had my house painted and paid my painter with 24 weeks of half priced daycare. It was much easier on my budget than paying $1400 up front, and I actually gave him $1680 in free childcare.

Be Creative. If the only credit card you have is for Home Depot, maybe your provider needs a new furnace or stove. It is still way better than not getting paid. Your provider will appreciate your honesty and the fact that you care enough to try and pay your bill in any way possible. We just want to know you value us as an employee, and care about the fact we have a mortgage payment and cell phone bill due every month just like you do.

You've Made Your Choice— Now do the Research

Once you decide on the final 2 providers you really like, it is time to do some research to find out everything you can about these individuals. Most parents rely on the state to do background checks that are thorough. This can be a costly mistake. Most states are on a very tight budget. They usually only run a minimal check which looks for child abuse charges or convictions in their state only. Very few states do a thorough national background check that includes not only child abuse, but other convictions which are relevant such as DUI or other criminal offenses. For example, if a person is convicted or pleads guilty to a felony domestic violence charge, they are supposed to be prohibited from doing childcare in Iowa for a minimum of 5 years. But if they have a suspended sentence, which means that if they do their probation with no further incident then the record is expunged, then a simple background check will not find record of the felony. There are providers in Iowa who slip through this loophole, and in one instance a provider was given a daycare registration less than one month after completing a year of probation for a felony that should have kept her from doing childcare in Iowa for a minimum of 5 years. Even though she pled guilty and had in fact committed the offense, because it was expunged it was not found. Ironically, nowhere on an application for a childcare license in Iowa does it even ask if you have ever been arrested or convicted of child abuse or any other kind of crime anywhere. Even video stores and grocers ask their employees this question, so why does the state of Iowa leave it out?

So where to start? First you need to ask this person for their date of birth, social security number and full name. If they have a problem with you running a background check, ask them if there is some reason they don't want one run. If they disclose that they have bad credit or other non-relevant issues, assure them that this is not what you are looking for. If necessary, take them a release which states what the background check is for and what you will be checking. There is one at the end of this chapter which you can copy and use.

Then begin with free public records. Most states have a database where you can find records pertaining to that state. There will be record of speeding tickets, DUI's and any state offenses, such as assault, theft and other crimes that are charged at the state level. Make sure you read the filings in order to find out what a charge actually is. Misdemeanor theft could be a check which bounced and wasn't picked up within 10 days. This isn't the kind of offense which would keep someone from being a bad childcare provider. In fact, since childcare providers often have to deal with receiving bad checks, it sometimes causes them to have bad checks. On one occasion a daycare client wrote an $860 bad check to our account. Since we didn't know it had bounced, our daycare had 5 checks returned before 48 hours was up. By the time we found out we were $1240 in the red. Since the family who bounced the check never made good and split, it took weeks for us to recover and pay all of the checks that were returned, because every day we had more bank fees and merchant fees. This is why most providers require money up front. The other issue that is irrelevant in my opinion is a credit report. Childcare providers depend on their clients to pay on time in order to pay their bills. You don't want to know what percentages of clients don't pay their provider on time. In addition, the worst clients for paying on time are government agencies, so if your provider takes daycare assistance she likely struggles to keep everything paid on time. The truth of the matter is that childcare is a very mediocre paycheck, and providers are never independently wealthy unless they have a spouse with a great job. So don't worry about whether she pays VISA on time, it won't make her love your child any more if she has a 750 FICO score versus a 510.

Here's what you do care about. Any kind of violent tendency is a no-go for a childcare provider. If there are any domestic violence or assaults, any criminal mischief, any convictions at all for drugs, DUI or any other indicators of substance abuse such as public intoxication, you should really evaluate how well you like this candidate. You can take into account how old the charges are, whether they were dismissed or she was convicted, the details of the case and you should most definitely ask for her side of the story. No-one has a perfect life, but childcare providers should be above reproach when it comes to their ability to keep calm under pressure and control their temper. If a loud mouthed woman in a bar can make them lose their temper and throw a punch, what effect are 3 screaming infants going to have on their psyche? And even if a provider will not be driving your children anywhere, a DUI is a sign of an alcohol problem. You need to address whether or not the provider recognizes this and has taken the necessary steps to get help.

The next records to check are federal. This includes federal charges such as welfare fraud, social security fraud and all other federal offenses. Once again, you don't care about a bankruptcy or IRS tax issues, unless they are current and it looks like her house is going to be sold. You care about signs that she will file fraudulent state bills on your behalf or indications she cannot be trusted with your Social Security numbers because she has been convicted of fraud or identity theft.

One of the most important records to check is sex offender records. Make sure no-one in her household is on the sex offender registry. If one of her close neighbors is, ask if she is aware and what steps she has taken to ensure your child's safety. She does not get to choose her neighbors, but you do get to choose whether or not your child is in daycare 1 block from a sex offender who favors your child's age and gender.

Last but not least make sure your provider has a current child abuse check on file with the licensing agency. If your state allows, ask to see her file and pay attention to any founded complaints. Remember that when a childcare provider terminates a family, often the first thing they do to get even is complain to the licensing agency in an effort to get her license revoked. Since they can file complaints anonymously and there is no fear of prosecution for filing a false report, angry neighbors, terminated employees and anyone else who wants to cause trouble can allege anything they want and the provider immediately gets inspected. You do want to pay close attention to violations that were founded and that the provider was notified about. If they are a paperwork violation such as a missing shot record, remember that the parent is responsible for these. If the violation is a safety issue such as open outlets during an inspection, make sure the

Co-Parenting Strangers

issues were marked as corrected on follow-up. If the complaint was for lack of supervision, such as a child out alone in the street and was marked founded, walk away. This is not the kind of supervision you want.

The best way to make sure you have chosen the right provider is to check their references. If you think it is a waste of time to check references you are wrong. Many parents tell me they don't check references because a provider would not give anyone who won't say great things about them. I completely disagree with this opinion. It is all about the questions that you ask when calling references. Here are some of the questions I like to tell parents to ask the people they are calling about their current provider. Assure the reference you are calling that you will not tell the provider who you called, and they don't have to disclose they were called unless they want to. Then ask the following:

1. What do you like the most about this provider?
2. What are things you don't care for?
3. Has there ever been a time you disagreed with this provider about the care of your child and how was the issue resolved?
4. How may personal or sick days have the provider taken in the last 12 months?
5. Have you been free to come and go in the daycare home as you please?
6. Have you been able to meet and communicate with the other daycare parents in the home?
7. Do you think this provider has a little or a lot of turnover?
8. Has your child ever been injured in this daycare? How and how was he/she cared for?
9. Does your child like going to this provider? Does he/she seem happy when you pick them up?
10. Do you have any concerns about this person?
11. Do you feel this provider would tell you if something was wrong?
12. How long have you been with this provider?
13. If you could change one thing about this daycare, what would it be?

These are the kind of questions that will get you a picture that is more accurate than just asking "would you recommend this person to watch my child?"

Always call at least 3 references. By taking notes you can begin to see a picture of the daycare. For example, if every client you call has been there less than 6 months, you know this provider changes families a lot, which is not a good thing. If they have been with her for years it is a great sign. If they all say they would make her more flexible about pick-up time and you have a job where you will be late often, maybe you aren't a match made in heaven. If you have a job where you cannot take off and they all agree she takes 1-2 days off a month, walk away. If they all know each other and half of them are related or work together, this is the best sign ever! It means that this provider is to the point where she does not have to even look for clients, they come to her based on rave reviews from friends and family who would not lie to them about the care they will be getting. Here's a story of how this can happen:

> *When I moved from Urbandale to West Des Moines I lost a couple of families because the drive was too far out of their way. I was a little worried about how I would fill the slots, but I shouldn't have been. I had been watching Art and James since they were little. The minute I moved their uncle, who was mom's brother, announced he and his wife were expecting. Since my new home was 2 miles from their house and his sister had been thrilled with the care of her two sons, they hired me 3 months into their pregnancy. Then his wife let her sister know and it just happened she needed care for her 4 year old son Nate. A few weeks later as it happened they were talking with a girlfriend they went to school with and a few days after that Dawson started. I went from having two members of the family's children to having 4 and a friend.*
>
> *Soon after moving I got hired by my lawn care guy to watch his grand-daughter. Within a month I was watching his girlfriend's grandson as well. Then I accepted the twin's mom's co-workers. I now had a waiting list for 2 years for an infant opening. The great thing was that communicating with all of them was easy, because once I told one they all knew. And when I needed my first day off in 6 years for illness, the ones who had days off took care of the other children, so no one lost any pay. At that point my*

> *daycare became a much more homelike place, with cousins and siblings and best friends all playing together under one roof.*
>
> *I now still have all those kids. I have 6 moms trying to get pregnant and one trying to adopt another little one. I don't think I will ever have to worry about being short on kids again. On the other hand, I hope I never tick one of them off, because I will lose 3-4 clients in a week.*

If you do not feel up to checking on this provider yourself, there are online companies that will do a check for $30-$100. We have listed some of these in the back section of this book.

After making all of the necessary inquiries, you can decide which provider meets your family's needs and feel safe leaving your child there because you know you have checked the provider out. If you think the recommendations in this chapter are overkill . . . This is a true story:

> *I always knew there were other providers who didn't do the best job. I was aware that there are providers out there that just do the bare minimum in order to keep the families they have. I did not realize how big of a problem there was in my city with providers who were guilty of neglect and abuse until my phone started ringing off the hook when several providers in my own neighborhood began being arrested. First was the provider who was watching over 20 children in a house with 900 square feet, while only being licensed to watch 6. Next was the provider leaving children sleeping alone and running errands during naptime? And then there was the nut who was arrested for fracturing a baby's skull and killing him.*
>
> *I had not met the provider who was a few blocks from me. I had heard she did daycare and some of my neighbors knew her and said she was super nice. When my phone started ringing on a Thursday night with parents asking about daycare, all the parents said was that they had to find someone immediately and could they set up an interview. I got 10 calls, agreed to 5 interviews and*

told the other families that if the ones who had interviews set up did not hire me I would call them back. I only had a maximum of 4 openings and I didn't really want to be completely full. I firmly believe being licensed for 16 does not mean you should watch 16, and I had been very comfortable with us having 12. But there was something about the way these parents sounded that made me want to meet them and at least try to help them.

As soon as I met with the first family the story started to come together. They were clients of the neighbor, and had been taking their children there for months. They said they had no reason to be concerned. Then on Tuesday their provider had called them and let them know she was ill and would be closed on Wednesday. They stayed home with their child on Wednesday, and on Thursday they dropped their children off and said goodbye. They all got to work and about 10AM their phones began ringing:

"Mrs. Johnson, this is Kay Smith from the Department of Human Services" the voice began. "We need for you to come and pick up your children from daycare. We are going to be revoking your provider's license, so you will not be able to bring your children back here until this is all resolved. I will explain everything when you get here but I need for someone to pick your children up right away." Immediately the parents began arriving at the daycare. As they arrived they saw their children sitting on the lawn with a lot of their children they did not know. Their provider had always met them at the door and taken their child from them. They had not been further than her living room ever and had no idea that she was watching 23 or more children by herself all day with no helper. There were children still in their car seats that had not been taken out or changed since they arrived. There were even a couple of children who were obviously disabled. When they asked for their children, they were asked to fill out their name, address and phone number. They were asked if they knew the other children, because there were some children who did not have paperwork and the childcare provider had not given any information about who they were or how to contact their parents. They told DHS they did not know the other kids and took their

children and left. The next day they received a notice in the mail that their provider's license was being revoked and that she would be prohibited from doing childcare in Iowa for a minimum of five years.

As I listened to the families tell their story I felt terrible. How could we not have known? I don't spend a lot of time with my neighbors but didn't anyone see how many children were going through her front door? When I got inspected a month later I asked the worker what had happened. I was told they were still finding more families and that she had been charged with child endangerment. The worker said they had come to inspect and she refused to let them in. They informed her they would return the next day and left. The next day they arrived (Wednesday—the sick day) to find she had 4 kids. The worker was suspicious and the next morning DHS came back again, this time with an officer and a warrant. When they got into the back of the house, they found a couple dozen children in one small room. There were kids everywhere and they were dirty and unchanged. There were no other adults in the home and when they asked the provider confirmed she did not have a staff. When they checked her license on the wall, it was for 6 kids. I took four children that had come from this daycare home and they all had issues. They were aggressive from having to fight other kids for food and toys, they were developmentally delayed and they had a hard time adjusting to the structure in our home.

Two months later I got a call from a mom who had caught her provider putting the children down for a nap and then going shopping. Her 4 year old had been coming home telling her that Miss May would leave them all alone and she didn't want to go there anymore. The first time she said it mom blew it off, but after a few times it got hard to ignore. So one morning she dropped her child off at the daycare and parked around the corner. She called work and told them she would be in late, but if anyone called to tell them she was in a meeting. Then she sat and waited. After a few hours her provider came out and got in her car and drove away—with no children! Mom called the police and within minutes they were banging on the door. They could see the children asleep in the floor in the living room, but no adults. Twenty minutes later the provider came back. She saw the police and tried to sneak in the back, but was caught at the back door. The children were sent home and she was arrested. Turns out she was giving them Benadryl to get them to sleep. The four year old I got from there was a complete joy. I will never understand how someone could drug her and then leave her alone for personal errands.

The last fiasco was a few months later. A baby received a skull fracture and died in daycare. The provider was convicted. I inherited 2 little boys from this daycare home. They have been wonderful. By all reports this provider had been a good caregiver for a long time, and then just snapped. No-one had an insight into what happened.

One of the great things about having over 20 years of experience is that I get referrals a lot from DHS and Childcare Resource and Referral. One of the bad things is that I am the first to get a call when another provider does not do the job they have promised to. Unfortunately when daycares get shut down, often it is simply an issue of DHS revoking a license. It rarely makes the paper unless a child is injured or killed, and often the provider is allowed to go back to doing daycare after a period of time, or they choose to be a non-registered provider after their registration is taken from them. Parents who interview these providers have no way of knowing about what happened without requesting complete information from DHS about the provider and the address. The best way to know about your provider is to check all references, check the courts and ask the right questions. Pop in unannounced a couple of times to see where your child is and what they are doing. And trust your gut.

Building a Trust Relationship

When your new caregiver begins watching your children, you probably won't know much about them. You won't know their favorite color, their hopes and dreams or their bad habits. More importantly, you won't know their parenting style. It is crucial that you choose a provider that is like you in parenting style. If you are a sixty's style crunchy parent who uses cloth diapers and wants organic food for your child and your provider is a militant structure buff/ germ freak, the two of you will get along about as well as two male beta fish (you know, the pretty ones that live in little cups and look friendly but kill each other when put together?) in one tank. In other words, bad choice!

No provider is going to do everything just the way you like it. There are however a list of things that you can do to make things go smoothly. In the beginning it is important to talk with your provider up front about things you feel strongly about. Here are a few of the things you need to discuss up front and be willing to negotiate. Along with each item are hints on ways to help your provider to accommodate your needs.

Talk #1: If you have religious beliefs that may enter into the daycare relationship or affect how your provider does her job, you have to let her know up front. The best example of this is a Muslim family going to daycare in a Christian home where bacon is served up every morning. Another example would be 7th day Adventists, who never accept blood products. The best way to handle these issues is simple. You handle them for your provider. If you are Muslim, provide your sitter with non-pork frozen or fresh meals to serve to your children on the days the other children eat pork. You can provide her with all beef hotdogs or sausage; you can give her bags of frozen chicken nuggets, anything easy for her to fix your child at the same time as she is making food for the other children. You will also need to provide her with a pan to fix your child's food in if you are strict about cooking in pans that have never touched pork. Most of all, don't forget to give her a list of all the things which have pork by-products in them, such as jelly beans, because she will probably not be educated about halal food. If you are 7th day, make sure you give your sitter a witnessed, notarized authorization for medical care with a special directive attached explaining your beliefs and the care you do and do not want given to your child in your absence. It would not be right to ask your daycare provider to ever have to decide whether or not to allow your child to be given blood in a life or death situation and it is your responsibility to protect your religious beliefs. In addition it is a good idea to make sure you have copies of your directive in your child's file at their doctor's office and the hospital you use. So think about any aspect of your religion that might need to be addressed during daycare and make a plan with your provider. If you don't believe in God at all, choose a provider who will honor your atheism.

Talk #2: Dietary Restrictions: Are you a sugar phobic? Is your child Obese? Are you a crunchy mom who only wants organic? And let's not forget about those zany vegans and vegetarians (and there is a big difference) who feel like they will be able to hear your arteries groaning if you eat a Big Mac (yum!) Once again be up front and be willing to buy the organic foods and sugar free, gluten free whatever free foods.

Talk # 3: Environmental: How much TV is too much? Are you for or against pac-n-plays? Do you want your provider to put your child in cloth diapers? What about napping? Just a hint . . . . Yes you do want your child to have a nap. Seriously.

Talk# 4: Family problems that may intrude: This talk is for couples who are in the middle of an ugly divorce. It is for single parents who have custody or foster parents who are bringing their foster children to daycare. It is also for couples who have family members that they do not want seeing their children. It is especially important whenever there are legal papers involved. Chapter 8 covers your provider's legal responsibilities and is a chapter you have to read if this situation applies to your household.

Talk# 5: Medical Issues: It is absolutely your responsibility to educate yourself and your childcare provider about any physical, mental or emotional disability or illness your child may have. There are a couple of great ways to do this. First buy your provider books on the subject or print them information off the internet. If you bring your provider medications for your child, make sure you bring her the pamphlet that lists all of the possible side effects and reactions so that she can watch your child for them. If it is at all possible you should always be with your child when they take a new medicine for the first time, for at least an hour. Another great way to help your provider would be to find a local seminar or support group dealing with your child's illness and offer to take her at your expense. The two of you can learn together and bond over an evening of education.

Talk #6: Your job: If you have a regular 9-5 bank job where you close on time and it takes 5 minutes to get out the door you don't need to have this chat. If you are a sales rep who has to finish a sale even if it runs you over your hours by a ton—you need to talk to your provider. Ask how she feels knowing you may not be able to call her until right before you are due to show up and have a back-up plan for who will pick up your child. If you are a firefighter or police officer, give your provider a list of people to call and discuss how late you will be before she begins calling them. Things could go very wrong in your line of work, and your provider may be the first person to catch on. She needs to have a plan for your child.

Talk# 7: Your support system: If you are a single parent with no family or friends nearby, or a couple where one of you travels, talk to your provider. Ask her how she would handle an emergency if something happened to you and discuss with her how long she would be willing to keep your child if there was a problem and someone had to come from a long distance to get your child. You do not want your child turned over to DHS simply because you have a car accident and your sitter closes @ 6 with no exceptions.

Talk #8: The contract terms: Any good childcare provider will have a handbook outlining both of your responsibilities. If there is no paperwork you should be very skeptical. The handbook should cover a lot of different items. In fact it is so complex there is an entire chapter dedicated to it. But this is your reminder that you need to ask any questions you have right up front. The number one cause of problems between providers and their clients is miscommunication.

OK—those are the basic discussions that should be gotten out of the way during the final meeting before your child starts. If you can, try to make it a pleasant meeting over coffee or sodas and do not bring your child along for two reasons. First, you don't want to have to deal with caring for your child while discussing crucial points and secondly your child should not be privy to you talking about them in a frank and honest manner.

It is always a good idea to talk honestly about your family. Your child will tell your provider things you probably would never share on your own. They will repeat things you talk about at home, and they will confide in their daycare provider when you and the hubby are squaring off over the dinner table. Here's a prime example:

> *Marcus can't keep anything at home. Every morning he fills us in on what mom and dad have to say about us, about each other and about the price of tea in China. Mom is not a very positive person and sometimes the things she says about us are not so complementary. "My mom says you should clean me up better at the end of the day because I can't go out in public looking gross" he chirps, "and my dad told my mom she better get another job because she likes shoes". The funniest ever was a day dad showed up to pick Marcus up early. In front of 4 other parents and 7 kids, Marcus patted his dad on the back and asked in a very loud tone "Daddy, does your penis still hurt?"*
>
> *Dad immediately answered "No Marcus I'm fine".*
>
> *Even louder Marcus shrills "I know . . . if your balls are all better then we can go for a bike ride!"*
>
> *Dad was red clear up to his hairline. He muttered quietly "I had a procedure yesterday to ensure that Marcus is the last blessing in our household. His mother doesn't think sometimes what he might repeat when she says it." He grabbed Marcus's hand and backpack and hauled Marcus out the door.*

It was weeks before we saw dad again, but the minute I saw him I could hear that little voice in the back of my head wondering if he was as embarrassed as he looked. I didn't have the heart to tell him we were way past hearing about his penis and were now hearing about him cutting up the credit cards and throwing out mom's shoes.

The moral of the story is that if you are going to talk about things you don't want us to know (like how derelict you think we are) don't discuss it in front of your child.

Once you have sat down with your new provider and covered all of your needs, make sure you are listening to their response. Watch their body language. If it becomes clear they are uncomfortable be ready to make some decisions. A provider may want a new client very badly, and be willing to agree to things she might not if she had more money coming in. Remember that to you this is a life changing event and to them it is just a job interview.

Last of all, make it clear that you will always be honest with your provider even when the topic is unpleasant and that you hope they will do the same. Make sure you tell them the good and bad points about your child and your family, but no excuses please. Here is a chart for what your excuses sound like to us.

"She is spoiled, but I was older when I had her and she is my miracle baby": This means your little angel will pull hair, scream and throw huge fits for attention and instant gratification.

"Our last provider claimed he was being mean, but we never have that problem at home"

Loosely translated this is an only child with no-one to be mean to at home.

You say active-we hear the prefix hyper.

You say inquisitive—we run to check the cabinet locks and safety gates.

Theresa J. Mulhern

You say perfect little angel—all of a sudden we have no openings.

Providers want to know the honest deal. Tell us if your child has violent crying spells and what you do to calm him. Tell us if your daughter likes to eat off the floor, we need to know.

Be sure to tell us the good things about your child. If there are things you are working on at home, such as toilet training or ABC's we can continue the learning at school if we are aware. If your child loves certain music or is an avid builder with wooden blocks this knowledge can help us build a relationship with them.

Being honest and communicating during the interview is only the first step. Trust is a long term feeling and is not given right away. Most parents will tell you they completely trust their childcare provider, and that they know the person watching their child always tells them the truth. Most providers will tell you exactly the opposite. Because no matter how much we want to believe our parents are trustworthy, experience has shown that even the very best of parents will bend the truth and even outright lie to preserve their own wants and needs.

Once you breach your provider's trust you will never get it back. If you lie to us for your own gain even once we will watch for you to lie all the time. Where we once upon a time would give you the benefit of the doubt, you lose the benefit of our generosity. We will stop going out of our way to help you, because you will have shown a lack of regard and caring for us. It's like finding out your husband lied to you so that he could do something for himself knowing it would cause problems for you.

We all know everyone tells white lies to save someone's feelings. That is not the kind of thing I am talking about here. So let's talk about some of the ways parents lie that cause providers to send them packing.

- Never tell your provider you are going to work when you aren't. We are here so that when you are working your child has a safe loving place to go. We aren't here for trips to the store, massage appointments, haircuts or shopping with the girls. We don't dump our children on others for these things. We not only take

Co-Parenting Strangers

our children with us sometimes we have to take yours. If you want to pay us extra and ask us to cover these things we will be happy to, but we don't want to feel like a foundling hospital. You are not paying for all the hours we are open; you are paying for the hours you have to be at work and can't be your child's caregiver. Dad can parent during your hair appointment. Aunt Suzy can babysit while you go to the gym. Better yet take your child with you. They cannot learn how to behave in public if you never take them anywhere with you. For health and safety reasons we have to know where you are. Yes we get you have a cell phone, but if you are in the gym and can't hear it, we don't know to call the gym and have you paged.

- When you bring your child to daycare knowing they are sick and lie to us about it you make us furiously angry. It is the ultimate act of cruelty and carelessness to expose your provider, her family and the other children in her care to an illness. You don't get to justify it by telling yourself your child got the virus from daycare. You can't make the excuse everyone else has already been exposed. And a cold for your child might mean hospitalization for a small infant or a child with Asthma. When your child tells us in circle time that they threw up at home, or that they had medicine for a fever, it is all we can do not to say very inappropriate things. And contrary to popular belief we are not stupid, and when your baby gets a high fever 3 ½ hours after arriving we know the Tylenol just wore off.
- Don't wait until the day your bill is due to tell us you can't pay us. Chances are you know well ahead of time that you are going to have a problem making your daycare payment. You would not want to go to work on payday and find out that your boss wasn't going to pay you, and that he had known all week. Tell us honestly if you are going to be late with our paycheck.
- If you find out your check has been returned we need to know the moment you do. We may have savings we can transfer so that we don't have bank fees or checks being returned. Since you will know the day it happens, waiting for us to call you is unacceptable.
- Imagine you are just waking up in the morning and having your first cup of coffee. Then imagine all of a sudden you are

teleported to work still in your pajamas. You haven't gotten your kids up for school yet and suddenly you are tied to your desk. That is exactly what you do to your provider when you show up an hour early unannounced. We live at our office, but this does not mean we are open 24/7. Stick to the schedule you hired us for.

- Don't ever tell us your child has a medical condition in order to get something you want. Over the years I have watched a parent lie about her child having asthma in order to force us to provide nebulizer treatments every time he got a cold. I have seen a mother claim her children were allergic to fish simply because she did not like the smell, and one mom informed us her child was lactose intolerant in order to try and convince us to give her child soy milk because she herself was vegan, and did not want to get a doctor's note. Don't claim ADHD to excuse bad behavior, unless you have an actual diagnosis.
- Don't make your pediatrician write a doctor's note for something that is not medically necessary. Your child does not have a medical need for a blanket in their crib. They do not need triple portions of food and they don't need Tylenol for teething for weeks on end.
- Never give your child medicine without telling us. We get scared when a child is groggy and confused, and if we knew they had allergy medicine before coming we would be less concerned. All medicines can have serious side effects or allergic reactions.
- Passive-Aggressive tactics are not conducive to trust. If something is upsetting you the best way to handle it is with honesty and an open mind. Sly and underhanded comments are not the way to let us know you don't feel your child is being cared for.
- Negative comments about your provider to the other families in care are the best way to get yourself booted. Address your issues with us. The other families can't make changes in care for you and we won't appreciate being badmouthed before even being asked about an issue.

You might think that I am being melodramatic. There is no joke here. You and your children are in our lives in a major way. You are in our home where we live. You overhear private conversations and see us argue with our children and our spouse. If we have process servers or bill collectors contacting us you will know, and you may even be the one who finds the disconnect notice on the door when our water bill is late. We don't get the same kind of personal view into your business, so we are extending a trust that is huge. We trust you not to judge, not to gossip and not to assume. We have no way of knowing when you hire us if you will look for new daycare the first time we don't live up to your expectation when it comes to the cleanliness of our house or the behavior of our children. We have faith that the only thing that matters is the care we give your child, and not the fact you don't care for our teenager's mouth.

We also extend trust to you in other ways. We trust you not to place our children in harm's way. We trust that you will support our decisions when it comes to discipline. We trust that you will come and tell us honestly when there is an issue, and not let it fester and grow until you fire us. If you decide to find new care, we trust you will give us notice so that we can replace the pay and that you will be honest about why you are leaving.

Last of all, we trust you will pay us for our time. We trust you will understand that we are the bill that should be paid above all others. Without childcare you cannot go to work.

As your provider we owe you certain commitments as well. We need to be honest if there is an issue. We need to tell you if our child is ill, because we cannot keep our child home without them being in the same home with yours. We should never give your child medicine without telling you first. We should never take your child anywhere without your knowledge or consent and we should never leave your child in the care of someone else without your permission.

You should treat your provider with the same honesty and respect you would expect from your spouse. This is a very close and long term relationship. The goal should be to have your child with the same caregivers until kindergarten and even longer if you need before and after school care. Children do the best when they have long term relationships with loving adults. Children who are bounced from childcare to childcare lose trust, and are less likely to bond and have strong ties with caregivers because they don't see them as long term.

If ever you have a question about whether or not to do something, ask yourself a simple question. If someone handled the situation this way and I was the provider, how would I feel and why? If you would not be happy about it then it is a bad idea.

Your Provider's Legal Obligations

On the surface it seems very simple. You pay someone to watch your child. You drop off in the morning and you pick up in the evening. If you knew all of the things that could go wrong you would not be able to function. There are some legal issues that have to be talked about in order to understand why your provider can't always say yes to you. To begin with, we should discuss all of the legal bodies your provider answers to and what they do that affects your child's care.

Your provider receives a license or registration from the State DHS or ACF office. They are in charge of conducting spot checks and licensing inspections. They have licensing regulations that providers have to comply with concerning every aspect of care from diaper changing to rest time. If your provider is inspected and is not in compliance they not only risk losing their license they risk being charged with child neglect or abuse. Here are a few examples.

* In Iowa blankets are not allowed in cribs. Neither are mobiles, pillows or toys. Parents wanting their child to sleep with a blanket will insist over and over, and will even resort to a doctor's note. The provider still can't comply.
* Sunscreen, diaper cream and lotion are medications. They cannot be applied without a written consent form listing the name, dosage and application instructions. They also cannot use diaper cream on a child that doesn't have a diaper rash. In some states even Desitin requires a note from a physician.
* Providers are required to adhere to strict guidelines for medicines. They cannot give your child nebulizer treatments on your say-so. They have to have all medicines in the original container clearly

marked with a current fill date and dosage instructions. They cannot alter the dosage or the schedule. This rule makes parents crazy, because they often want for us to administer 2 doses closer together so that they don't have to do it at home, and we can't. If a medicine says 2x per day they need to be 12 hours apart, not 8. Providers cannot accept old prescriptions or re-use a medication from one illness to another. Every time a nebulizer is used a new doctor's note must be given and can be valid for no more than 1 week. It is very frustrating for providers when parents demand breathing treatments multiple times per day and insist we give them even if their child has no symptoms, while the doctor's order states the medicine is to be given "as needed". Nebulizer sticks must be in the package with the child's name on it. You cannot bring us a handful of loose sticks and expect us to give them to your child.

* A provider can be held liable for releasing a child into the custody of someone who does not have an appropriate car restraint system (car seat). So if you forget the booster seat at home and put your three year old in a seatbelt, we are required by law to report it to DHS.
* Providers must keep children safe. We cannot allow children to be removed from care during a tornado or severe storm warning.
* A provider can be held liable for releasing a child into the custody of a parent who is under the influence of any mind-altering medications to include pain killers, cough medicines, anti-anxiety medications and more. If they feel the adult is impaired, there is an obligation to notify the other parent and if the parent insists on removing the child the provider is obligated to call the police.
* Any claims, assertions signs or symptoms of abuse observed or reported to the provider have to be reported to DHS under mandatory reporter laws. No matter how much we like a parent and even if we think it was non-intentional, marks on a child made by the parent lasting more than 24 hours have to be reported.
* A provider has limits on the number of children they may have at any one time. They cannot accept your child into care on a day they are not scheduled if it puts them over. They cannot accept your child early or keep your child late if other children

have not yet left or will be arriving before you pick-up. In other words, you have to stick to your schedule and you have to ask to change it, not just show up 3 hours early and expect us to welcome you.

* Infants under 12 months must be on formula or breast milk. Your provider cannot switch your child to cow's milk at 9 months, even if you demand it. We cannot replace formula with food either. We know it is expensive, but your child needs it until 1 year of age.

* We cannot give your child soy or almond milk instead of cow's milk unless you have a doctor's note every year stating they cannot have it.

* In the case of separated or divorced parents, we cannot disclose information about one to the other. Jack does not have the right to know if his ex-wife Susan paid her bill on time, or if she was late picking up. Susan cannot insist we collect fees from Jack when she is the one who signed the childcare agreement and he did not. If Susan authorizes her boyfriend to pick up her son, Jack has no standing to forbid it without a court order.

* We have no right to ever withhold a child from one parent based on orders from the other. Once the child's records have been filled out listing a father or mother, that information does not get removed simply because mom broke up with dad and now wants to pretend he never existed. We do not get involved in whose turn it is to have the kids unless we have a certified copy of the custody order and the custody order states the exchange will take place at childcare. Both parents have equal legal standing at all times until a judge says otherwise and we are in possession of the order. If you fail to provide us a copy we are not bound to comply with it based on your say-so.

* Providers are required to place infants on their back to sleep. They cannot allow infants to sleep in a car seat, bouncy or swing. So if you don't have your child on their back in a crib at home, you cannot be angry when they don't get restful sleep at daycare, because the rules are right there on the state website for you to read.

* Children have to have outside play time. Unless we have a doctor's order we cannot keep your child in for recess. In

inclement weather we have to keep them inside even if you object.

* Children are required to have rest time. Forcibly keeping them awake or forcing them awake while they are sleeping is considered abuse. So don't ask a provider to deny your child a nap or wake them after 30 minutes. If they need to sleep they will, and we will not deprive them of rest.

Besides DHS providers who participate in the food program have guidelines from them as well. There are rules about minimum serving size and what foods are credible. For example, each child must have a serving of all five food groups for lunch, so we cannot give your child mac and cheese every day just because that's all they want. We cannot water down juice even if you ask, and they have to have milk to drink with every meal.

In addition to DHS and the USDA, your provider has to comply with city occupancy and fire code laws. These laws include citations for parents who park with the backside of their car hanging out into the street, or pulling onto the grass because they don't want to park up the street. There are even laws about how many parents can arrive or pick up per hour, and dropping off early and picking up late can cause your provider to get a hefty fine and perhaps lose their permit.

Last of all there is the health department. Your provider is required to report exposure to certain illnesses such as pertussis and then notify all of the parents. There are regulations about what types of cleaners can be used and how the dishes need to be watched. You may hate the smell of bleach but your provider is required to use it. We cannot substitute organic or homemade cleaners.

In addition to all of the regulatory agencies, providers are also bound by the terms of their insurance policies. If their childcare is covered under their homeowner's policy it may only cover 3 children. If there are 6 children in the home and an accident or loss occurs, it will not be covered. Losses will only be covered during regular business hours, so if a parent uses the provider for care after hours, they need to be informed that the childcare insurance will not be in effect.

As if all of these weren't enough, providers always have to worry about civil liability. If a child gets ill because a provider allowed a child who was sick to stay instead of sending them home, can she be sued for the medical bills and lost wages? What about allowing a child who bites to continue biting another child over and over without terminating care?

There are many ways that you as a parent can compromise your provider and place unwanted liability on them. Here are just a few:

- Never bring your child through the door with food. You do not know what kind of allergies the other children in care may have. If your child shares their donut and another child with a peanut allergy dies, your provider loses everything over your bad judgment.
- Your childcare provider has checked every toy in her home for choking hazards and safety recalls. She hasn't checked every toy in your home. Keep your child's toys at home or in your car.
- Never medicate your child and drop them at daycare without informing your provider. If your child has a bad reaction to the medicine we won't even be watching for it. If they get hurt we will not have the right information to give the hospital. Worse still, even though medicine helps the symptoms it does not prevent your child from making other children sick. If your child needs medicine to function they need to be home where they can be properly monitored and cared for.
- Never lie to your provider about going to work so that you can leave your child. In an emergency we have to know where you are. We cannot be hunting down a parent who is playing hooky while dealing with a fire.
- Never let your child out of the car or out of the daycare provider's front door by themselves. You need to be with them holding their hand. Even if you didn't hold them responsible for your child getting hit by a car, the news headline "Child hit by car at little tykes childcare home" will damage her business for years.
- Do not encourage your child to interact with your provider's pets. Even the best of dogs gets anxious with ten loud children in their face. If you allow your child to maul and molest the dog

- or cat at daycare then you are asking for your child to be bitten. Living in the daycare home does not make that dog a daycare toy. Your child may accidentally injure your provider's beloved pet, which is likely to cause some bad feelings.
- Tell your provider when your child gets injured at home. We have to know if your child hit their head or fell out of their crib. We cannot watch your child for symptoms if we don't know he has had an injury.
- Never leave your child in a vehicle in your provider's driveway. Either bring your child in with you or call from the drive so your provider can come out.
- Never leave a baby bag at daycare with anything in it but diapers and wipes. Another child could drink the infant Tylenol in the side pocket or find the extra lighter you keep in there. Your provider will be the one charged with lack of supervision. The best plan is a set of clothes and a pack of diapers and wipes, not even in a bag.
- Never place items in plastic sacks in your child's cubby. Another child could find the plastic sack and be suffocated.
- Never bring your infant or toddler to daycare with jewelry or small hair clips on. These items are choking hazards.
- Never ask your provider to medicate your child for something that is not an illness or injury. Giving Tylenol for days for "teething" can cause permanent liver damage and giving nebulizer treatments without medical supervision can cause heart problems.
- Never give your child or anyone else's hard candy or gum while at daycare. Wait until you get into your vehicle.

The best possible policy to follow is this. Personally walk your child to the door with nothing in his mouth, hands or pockets. Then at the end of the day you pick him up at the door and walk him to the car before giving him anything. Let your provider decide what is safe for all the kids at daycare.

Your Parental Responsibilities

Over the years there have been countless parents who have taken their child out of bed and thrown them in the car, pajamas and all. They then fling them at their daycare provider with the same diaper on from the night before and expect the daycare provider to have time to change, dress and feed their tired child while getting five more children through the door.

Childcare providers like to be able to greet each parent every morning and have time to answer questions and discuss relevant topics such as the last time an infant ate and how much sleep the two year old who is teething got. The best way to ensure your provider has a calm start to her day is to prepare yourself and your child before you leave your home.

The very best way to prepare is to start the night before. If you take a baby bag to daycare, check it each night when you get home and place it by the front door. Or pack it with a week's worth of items and leave it with your provider from Monday to Friday. Some providers prefer that everyone simply bring a large bag of diapers, one outfit and a can of formula. This may be due to the space in their home, so don't feel offended if you are asked to simply restock as needed. Be sure to pack the following items if you are packing a bag every day.

1. Formula: Although you should have a can at your provider's house, there may come a time when she runs out the day before and forgets to tell you because pick-up time was a zoo. Keeping a spare container, even a small one, will help her if she needs an emergency supply and will also provide a supply for you if you need to go somewhere directly from daycare.
2. Diapers: You should have enough diapers in your bag to get through your daycare day and 4 hours beyond in case of

emergency. For children up to 6 months, this equals 10 diapers for a full day. For 6-12 months you'll need 8 diapers. For over one year old, 6 diapers should be adequate. When your child is in Pull-ups pack 4 per day. These numbers are only accurate if you use a good quality diaper. If you buy cheap diapers in an effort to save money you will need to add extras. In addition your provider will not be happy about the frequent leaks that come with cheap diapers. Care enough to buy a great quality diaper and pinch pennies somewhere else. If you can't decide on a brand ask your provider which she prefers.

3. Spare clothes: Don't just fling a stained jumper into a bag and call it good. I know there is a feeling that if you send a cute outfit to the sitter's you won't be able to put it on your child when you want to. Go to a department store and buy an outfit or two from the clearance rack. Buy them a little large so that you don't have to replace them very often. These can then become your daycare spares and your sitter will have something decent to put on your child. If your child never has to use them (fat chance!) you can give them to your local shelter with the tags still on. Also, throw a couple of storage bags in to put wet clothes in for the way home.

4. Personal items: If your child uses a pacifier, pack 2 of them in case one goes missing. *Don't pretend like you don't lose them at home!* If your child has a runny nose, be sure and pack a bulb syringe for them. Do not pack medicines in a baby bag! You would not want another child getting a hold of medications out of your child's bag. Hand any medicines directly to your provider so they can be put up out of reach, even over the counter medicine like Tylenol. Mark your bulb syringe, sippy cup and pacifiers with your child's name in sharpie.

5. It is OK to pack one comfort item in your child's bag. Try not to fill it with toys that could get lost or broken at daycare. It is also OK to pack things you will use at the end of the day. For example, if you know you will be running errands after work, pack an empty sippy cup or bottle that your provider can fill for you as you are going out the door. Some small packs of snacks might also be helpful. Never pack something that needs to stay

cold and assume your provider will find it. Some of us never look in the baby bags that sit in our house every day.

OK, the bag is packed and ready to go. Now you need to prepare your child. Here are some tips for getting ready.

Make sure your child gets a good night's rest. Tired cranky children are a daycare nightmare because they become cranky and aggressive with other children. So do the work it takes to put your child to bed on time.

In the morning, get a fresh diaper on your child before going out the door. Your provider may be very busy getting children through the door, and she may not check on your child's diaper for up to an hour. If your child is in a diaper they went to bed in, they may get a rash or leak all over their clothes and the provider's furniture.

If you cannot dress your child in the morning, make sure to put clothes and shoes in a bag. Providers don't like to take children outside to play in their pajamas with no shoes.

Make sure to feed your child something in the morning. It can even be a granola bar or pop-tart in the car on the way. Your provider will not be able to sit your child down to a meal until all the kids arrive. Whatever you do, do not take your child through the daycare door with food or drink in their hands in front of the other children. You would not want other children eating in front of your child. Please be considerate of how hard it can be for your provider when every child she watches is hollering for the pop-tart your child has in their hand.

Last but not least, talk to your child about daycare. Explain to them that just like mommy and daddy go to work, they get to go and play with their friends until mom comes to pick them up. Let them know the day will go by quickly and that you will be back to get them. Try not to make a big scene or reward them for crying at the door. The best solution is to tell them goodbye with a smile and walk out, especially if they are having drama in an effort to get attention from you. Be short but sweet and leave quickly. Chances are they will try this for a few days and then quit.

If you encourage the behavior, your child will be crying at the door for months.

In addition to you and your child being prepared for daycare each day, it is your responsibility to make sure you keep your daycare provider apprised of any changes in your schedule or workday events. For example, if you decide to change cell phones, write your new cell phone number down and call your provider with it before you forget. If you change offices at work and your extension changes, let your provider know.

Absolutely if you are going to be gone from work for any reason you need to let your provider know in case there is an emergency with your child. If you have a cell phone there should be no problem. If you are going to be somewhere that you cannot be reached, such as a meeting, let your provider know and give her instructions who is to be called if something happens while your child is in her care. Although you may be confident nothing could ever happen, it only takes one true emergency to cause serious problems.

> *A friend of mine had been doing daycare for years. She was clean, organized and great with the kids. The one thing she didn't do was update her paperwork once a year with each of her families. She just trusted that if there were any changes they would let her know.*
>
> *After putting the 6 kids she watched down for nap one day, she went in 30 minutes later to find that one of the 2 infants in her care had passed away. It was later determined the baby had died of SIDS.*
>
> *The trauma of finding one of her daycare children dead was more than Tina could handle. After the paramedics came she began trying to reach all of her parents to have them pick up their children. By the time she finally reached someone for each child it was 2 hours later. Out of 6 families she only had the correct phone number for 2 parents. So in addition to dealing with ambulances, paramedics, the family of the child who had passed away and her own children who were completely traumatized by*

> *the events going on in their home, Tina had to search for parents who by the grace of god were the ones whose children were fine.*
>
> *Tina quit that day and has not done daycare since. I began renewing paperwork every year after that happened. God forbid I ever have to locate all of my parents because something so awful has happened, but if it does I want to be prepared.*

There may come a day your provider needs to find you not because something has happened to your child, but because someone else's child has been hurt. You don't want to add to the burden on her by forgetting to let her know about changes in your contact information. Providers live by the emergency list that hangs by their phone. Make sure your information is correct on that list. If your provider does a contact drill once per year, don't be disgruntled about her testing the emergency broadcast system.

In order raise a respectable adult there is a saying that it takes a village. This is partially true. Many parents feel that it is the job of the childcare and school to educate their child. No-one is responsible for your child unless they volunteer for the job. If you don't show an interest in your child's education, chances are they won't excel in school. If you don't pay attention to how they are doing in school there will be no-one to catch on when they fall behind.

Your childcare provider will teach your child along with the other children in her care. She is not a private tutor, so making demands that she work with your child on additional subjects is not appropriate when you can make the time to supplement at home.

Your provider should be willing to sit down with you once every six months to discuss how your child is doing developmentally. Is she on track for her age? Remember that your provider is a much better judge of how your child is doing, not because she knows your child better than you do, but because she has a much broader knowledge base. Your provider has dozens or hundreds of other children to compare developmentally, as well as extensive training in child development and the stages of learning.

Every parent thinks their child is brilliant and exceptional. Over the years we have had hundreds of parents of average children insisting their child is gifted and talented. The first few times we tried in vain to be honest and make them understand that there is nothing wrong with their child developing at a normal pace. There is an urgent need with these parents to have their child pushed ahead and taught to perform on command. They demand potty training start before their child is talking and that reading and writing lessons begin before the age of three. They buy programs like "Your baby can read" and don't understand they are simply playing "Monkey see Monkey do" with their child because the entire program is watch and repeat with no real cognitive learning happening.

There is an order to everything in life, and learning is no exception. Your child cannot learn to read until they can recognize the letters of the alphabet, capital and lower case. They cannot learn to write until they know what they are writing. It is futile to try to toilet train a child who cannot tell you when they need to go. And you cannot teach math to a child who doesn't recognize numbers.

A child's mind is like a sponge, but the trick is to teach them cognitive skills and they will learn forever. Memorization is not learning. Copying is not learning. Your child has to be interested and ready to process actual information. There are cues your child gives off that they are ready to learn a particular skill, and your provider is experienced at recognizing them. The very best practice is to work on the same curriculum at home that your child is working on at daycare. Trust your provider to teach in a logical order and to know when your child is ready for the material.

You have responsibilities when it comes to your child's education that has nothing to do with lesson plans and start when your child is very small. Here is a list in chronological order of the most important things you can do to raise a brilliant child.

From birth to one year you should:

1. Talk to your child using normal adult speech. Your child needs to learn how words should sound so that they can learn diction and pronunciation. It does not matter what you talk about, as

long as your child hears words and can begin to decipher the code we call communication. Use normal expressions, not crazy exaggerated clown faces.
2. Put your child down. Infants need to learn physical skills at an alarming rate. In a span of 12 months they learn to sit up, roll over, crawl and then walk. They learn to grasp and hold. They learn to turn their head to look at you and then to turn it when they hear a sound from the other direction. They learn to wave and clap and dance to music. If you are constantly holding your child or carrying them around in some contraption they cannot do any of these things. In order to roll over they have to be lying down. They cannot practice crawling in your lap. The more time you give your child on a blanket on the floor the faster they will develop these skills.
3. Put your child to bed in a crib and leave the room. Children need REM sleep even more than we do. It is during deep sleep that their body recharges to support extreme physical growth and change. Your child cannot achieve deep sleep in a vibrating seat or a swing. In addition sleeping in a seated position places pressure on a growing spine. Your child needs to sleep on a firm mattress on their back in a quiet room. You should get your child used to going to bed awake and falling asleep in the crib and not in your lap or on your chest.
4. Read to your child every day. Yes your daycare provider will read to them, but remember your job is to support and continue the learning they are doing during the day. Once again, it does not matter what you read, so pick out a great self-help or educational book you are interested in and read it for both your benefit. You can learn how to sew and make your child smarter all at the same time. And while they are on their blanket learning to crawl, you can be sewing adorable outfits for them to crawl in.
5. Expose your child to music. Turn off the TV and turn on the Beethoven and Bach. Studies show that children are mentally stimulated by music, especially classical music. There are companies like Brite music that make music that teaches history, manners and measurement. There are all of the wonderful songs from Schoolhouse Rock, like 'Conjunction Junction'. Even though your child won't understand the topics they will have a

great time with the music and later on they will remember the words and use the information without even knowing how they got it.
6. Feed your child a diet rich in omega threes. Make sure you stick to breast milk or formula for at least 12 months and I recommend two years. Young toddlers do not eat a varied diet and cow's milk is for baby cows. Your child needs this extra brain food for as long as possible. So spend the money and fill that sippy cup with complete nutrition, and then anything else is just gravy. Think of it as your baby's protein shake, only better.
7. Smile laugh dance and sing. Your child's entire personality and disposition are formed by age three. Since we don't know how much is nature and how much is nurture, stack the deck in your favor and help your child grow up happy, optimistic and creative.

From age one to two years:

1. Leave the TV off. Now is not the time to start using an electronic babysitter. Read books every night about every topic you can find. This is the time to start going to story time at the library. It is the time to begin finding out what things interest your child and foster those interests.
2. Begin object recognition. Show your child ten new things every day and say the name over and over. This might sound complicated but you can find 10 new things in one book. Take Jack and the Beanstalk. You have beans, a beanstalk, a harp, a golden egg, a giant, a castle, a goose, gold coins, a farm and an axe.
3. Walk with your child at least 4 days a week. A short walk every evening of five minutes will help your child to prepare for winding down to go to bed. Let your child walk as soon as they are able, no one is in a hurry and this will help tucker them out for a good long night of sleep.
4. Count for fun. Count the crackers at snack. Count the socks in the sock basket. Count the cups on the counter. Pre math begins with your child being able to count to 100. By 2 they can easily be taught to count to 20.

5. Use pre-writing activities. Make letters in sand, shaving cream on a tray, cool-whip or pudding. Cut letters out of colored paper and put them on the walls.
6. Talk to your child about everything. Use the proper names for items like body parts. Your child may need to come and tell you they are being touched inappropriately, and they should be able to use the word vagina, not cookie or who-ha.
7. Teach your child manners. Teach them patience. Teach them respect for their elders and kindness to others. You are not your child's friend. You are the person who is responsible for making sure they grow up with a conscience.
8. Place limits. Structure and schedule are important to a child and make them feel secure, because they know what is coming. Enforce naptime, bedtime, mealtime and quiet time. For dinner make healthy meals instead of giving in with mac and cheese simply because it's what your child has a fit for.

No doubt you will have days when you want to just give in and avoid the tantrum. Don't do it. No provider wants to watch a child who whines and hangs on their parent and hits and screams to get what they want. We know which parents discipline by the way their child behaves when they show up. The funny thing is that we usually have no problem getting their child to behave during the day, because from the beginning we discipline and create boundaries and structure. We will have a great day with no tantrums and a well behaved child, and then the moment mom walks through the door that same child begins whining and throwing themselves on the floor demanding donuts for dinner. And when mom tells them she already has donuts in the car we shake our head and heave a sigh of disappointment.

Don't try to put the cart before the horse. Your child doesn't need useless programs that teach them to see a word and mimic a motion or sound. They don't need to watch TV, they need to watch you. Remember, you don't get a do-over. Your provider will know who is raising your kids. I once had a set of twins that sang TV jingles all day and quoted TV characters they should never have been watching. Both children were morbidly obese and struggled in school. Believe it or not their mom was a nurse and dad a psychiatrist, so there was no excuse.

Theresa J. Mulhern

Don't be offended if your provider tries to help you with your child as they are having that meltdown. If she gives you advice, you should think about taking it. Remember that she has raised many children and has the experience and know-how to make your life easier.

Choosing to hire In-House—
The Nanny or Au Pair

For some families, keeping the children at home in their own environment is a perk worth paying for. For some, because of odd work hours or an inability to find a provider who meets their needs, a nanny or Au Pair is a necessity. A nanny can be hired through word of mouth, advertising or an agency. An Au Pair is hired through an official Au pair organization. It is always wise to find out from the agency how well they do with placements. Ask for references for the agent and check with families they have found nannies for.

Before you even interview your first candidate, it is necessary to make up an imaginary list of what you want in a candidate and what you want for them to be able to do. Do you want them to cook for your children or just make sandwiches? Make a list of responsibilities, job perks and pay scales. List qualifications you are looking for, such as a degree in child development or being bilingual in Spanish or French.

> *Lanie was a fabulous employee for the most part. She did everything asked without complaining and genuinely seemed to care for the kids. She would take them to preschool, speech therapy and the doctor when necessary. Although she had use of our van at any time, she chose to drive her own car. When she first got hired we found out she had a ticket she was paying off for not having insurance. She assured us she had found new car insurance after we offered to put her on our insurance, because we needed her to be covered in case she had an accident while our children were in the car. We should have asked to see the policy, because about 9 weeks later she backed into the side of my husband's dodge*

> *avenger and did about three grand in damages. The look on her*
> *face as she came in to tell me said it all . . .*

There are so many things you won't learn about a person in a job interview. You won't learn anything about their work ethic. You won't know if they truly love children or if they simply need a job and are willing to say anything to get one.

Hiring a nanny is nothing like contracting with a center or home provider. When you hire someone to come into your home you are opening yourself and your family up completely to scrutiny by and vulnerability to a total stranger.

For this reason you should never hire a nanny in your home except through a reputable agency which will assume some of the liability and you should insist on a separate background check and drug screen in addition to their screening process.

Even after all of the checks, there needs to be a probationary period in place where you are free to terminate services with no reason or severance required. This period should be no less than 90 days in length and should have very strict guidelines. For example, 3 or more absences during the probationary period should result in immediate termination. Any falsification of information on the application or paperwork should be grounds for being fired.

Your expectations and your nanny's job duties must be laid out in writing and signed by both parties. You should pay for a full physical and require that a physician certify that your nanny is in top physical condition, and free from any communicable disease. You will need evidence of vaccinations including pneumonia and pertussis. Make sure that all lifting and physical requirements are written out and that your candidate certifies that she can and will perform them. Nothing is more frustrating than hiring someone and all of a sudden they have a bad back that was never discussed or disclosed prior to being hired. If you are going to cover your employee with health insurance you should ask if they are pregnant or planning on becoming pregnant. You are not required to cover them with maternity coverage, but if you aren't going to you need to let them know so that they can get it on their own if they need it. Do not begin benefits until the probationary period is up. Maternity leave should not be offered until two years after hire, and you can require they take short-term disability insurance if you offer it and that they use all sick and vacation time before receiving maternity leave pay.

If your child is special needs, you must have a care plan for your nanny that outlines your child's illness or disability. Include what to do in case of an attack (such as asthma) or episode (such as a seizure). Write out specific instructions for your child's medications and treatments including dosage, times to be given and what to do afterward, such as keeping them upright. If your child has therapy that they attend, take the nanny with and have her in the room learning about the different exercises so that she can do them at home with your child. Make sure she has all of the necessary tools and that she knows where they are kept.

Hiring a nanny in home means costs that double their actual salary. If you offer twelve dollars an hour your cost will be over twenty by the time you pay unemployment insurance, social security and any employer benefits. If you expect her to drive your children around then you will need to provide a car or provide gas money and verify her insurance.

You will need to pay for your nanny to go to any of the events you send your child to. You cannot expect her to pay her own way into the zoo. You will need to cover her meals during outings and any other expenses as well.

You need to carry liability insurance that covers employees in the home. Otherwise you will need to cover your employee with workman's compensation.

You may be faced with the decision whether or not to allow your nanny to bring her own child with her. In addition you may have friends who want to nanny share. Remember that every child is an increase in liability, and takes time away from your own child. Nanny sharing is fine, as long as the other family is paying not only their half of the nanny expense, but also the cost for feeding their child and the cost of the liability insurance. Make it legal and in writing, with both parties giving adequate notice if they decide to leave the arrangement.

When interviewing a nanny, listen carefully to how they talk about others. If they talk badly about others to you, chances are good they will talk badly about you to others. If they gossip on the phone, they will gossip to others about you. Absolutely in your contract there needs to be a confidentiality clause, making it clear that there are financial penalties for the disclosure of personal or financial information pertaining to your family.

You will need to have definite boundaries with regard to your home. For example, there should be no reason for the nanny to be in your bedroom or your personal belongings. There should be guidelines about having guests, the use of the home and cell phones, the food allowed and what is off limits etc . . . .

If you are leaving your nanny with an infant I urge you to use cameras and check in frequently. Schedule some play dates when you are at home at least part of the time, so that you can see how she interacts and bonds with your child.

If you want things done a certain way, you will need to train your nanny. Show her how you change your child, prepare bottles and food and clean your home. Have a journal you write in at night and she writes in during the day, so that each of you knows how the baby's done during the other person's shift. www.toddlertimetoo.com has one called the baby tracker that is perfect for passing information.

- It is acceptable to require modest attire while in your home. This includes clothing which is loose fitting so that your nanny can bend and squat to play with and pick up your child. There needs to be no cleavage showing, no bare stomach, no short skirts or shorts. The very best way to handle this is to supply your nanny with 5 sets of nursing scrubs, and have her leave them in your home. She can change when she arrives and wash her hands at the same time. This will cut down on perfumes, animal hair, dust and cigarette smoke which might be brought in on her clothes and cause allergies for your child. They can be laundered right on premises, and with 5 sets you can expect she will wear a clean set every workday. The cost will be $20-30 per set. You should also get her a set of soft slippers for in the house so there is no risk she will track hazardous materials in and it will minimize the injury should she step on your child. Remember that this person will give off an impression of your home when they answer your door, and they will be the one setting the example for your child how to dress. You also do not want to be paying for the $80 jeans your child gets juice on.

- It is good practice to have a family manual for your nanny that has all the relevant information she may need. Include an Emergency Medical Authorization Form and copies of your Driver's License and Insurance Cards. Also make sure there is a current picture of your child, fingerprints which you can do with your local police department for free and a lock of your child's hair in a baggie. Make a necklace for your child with your contact information (dog tag necklaces are great) and instruct the nanny that your child is to have it on anytime they go on an outing. Should your nanny ever get in an accident with your child or lose him, these items will help EMS and police locate you and help your little one get medical care or a ride to you in a squad car.
- Your nanny should have her own car seat for your child in her car. Then you won't need to remember to leave her one.
- Your nanny should have a 72 hour kit in the home and in the car.
- You should have emergency plans and do drills with your nanny. These drills should include not only fire and tornado/earthquake, but also unwelcome stranger, burglary, gas leak, lost child and auto accident. Your family book should have the numbers of everyone she might need to call including the water and electric company, the insurance company, your child's teachers and anyone else she may need to contact.

Daycare Etiquette

Childcare is a little more than a business relationship. Because of the loving nature of providers we tend to get close with the families we work for. Boundaries line can be blurred and it is very easy to overstep without even knowing it. There are a lot of niceties that should be observed and here is a list of several.

- It is appropriate for your provider to get a gift for your child, but it needs to be a reasonable one. The cost should be $50 or less and it should be something you approve of your child having. It is OK to tell your provider no to buying your 6 year old make-up if you don't allow it at that age. Ask her to let you know beforehand what she is getting to give you time to give approval.
- It is appropriate to give your provider a gift for birthday and Christmas. These should be $100 or less. It is OK to ask for suggestions and gift cards are fine. If you cannot give your provider her birthday off, try to give her a day off that week. Your provider should always have Christmas Eve and Christmas day off or be paid holiday pay, even if you do not observe.
- It is OK to talk with your provider about your faith and what you do or don't want your child to be taught about religion. If you don't mention you are Mormon and she teaches your children her Catholic prayers, then you have no right to be angry. It is not OK to force her to attend church or religious activities with your child. It is also not OK to ever tell her that her faith is wrong.
- If you are using a full-time slot, it is not OK to ask your provider for a reduction in rate because you stay home for a day. Imagine that your boss kept cutting your hours. Would you stay or look for a new job?

- It is not OK to ask your nanny or childcare provider to care for your child when they are sick. It is also not advisable because if she gets sick then you can't go back to work when your child is better. Children who are ill need to be with their parents.
- It is a great idea to give your provider a bonus twice per year. This bonus can be up to one week's pay, and should include a note letting them know what they have done that is above and beyond for your family.
- It is never OK to post or publish pictures or commentary about your provider or nanny on Facebook, family websites or elsewhere without their consent. If you have an issue with your nanny, writing about it on Facebook, your blog or My Space constitutes creating a hostile work environment, even if you don't mention her by name, and you could be sued.
- It is never acceptable for your provider/nanny to post pictures of your home, your children or any commentary about them on any form of blog, website or social media such as Facebook. Your child's safety is far too important to be letting the childcare provider display them for her friend's friends.
- It is acceptable to check your provider's social media and monitor it for as long as she works for you. This needs to be a condition of hire.
- It is acceptable to monitor your provider's neighborhood for sex offenders. Sign up through an online notification service and notify your provider anytime you receive information that an offender has moved in nearby.
- It is not acceptable to take your provider away from her family during off hours with lengthy phone calls about issues that can be discussed during daytime hours by way of a phone conference during nap-time. Knowing when your child last pooped is not an urgent issue, because you don't need to do any prep work before they poop again. You may want to know why your child got a time-out, but it can wait until morning. Feel free to send an email or text but keep your tone non-accusatory and then understand you may not get an immediate response. Keep texting during reasonable hours because some providers keep their phones by the bed in case their own children need them. We don't need to be woken from a sound sleep at 3 AM for a

text from a mom wanting to know when we will be teaching her two year old to read.

In addition to keeping an eye on things without being a stalker, there are ways to speak to your provider. Here are some things that should never come out of your mouth unless you already have new childcare lined up.

1. "I just wanted to find out if any of the other kids at daycare have been sick." This comment tells us your child is becoming ill and you are looking for a reason to dump them at our house because it is our fault. Here's the scoop. Even if another child in daycare had been ill, we cannot violate their HIPPA privacy rights to tell you. The most we can do is post an exposure notice on our door which tells you your child has been exposed to an illness. We cannot tell you which kids had it, and we cannot allow your child to expose the kids who don't yet have it.
2. "I know you don't allow XYZ, but I went and got a doctor's order for it." Your doctor doesn't give us orders. If we tell you no to something it means no. I won't give drugs for teething for weeks at a time no matter how many doctors order it.
3. "I think I know my child better than you do." This statement might be true, but we know children in the general sense far better than you do, and your child is probably pretty normal, which means we know what we are talking about. In addition, we are non-biased observers who are less emotionally attached, and we have more awake time to observe your child in a controlled setting than you do.
4. "Sorry I'm late, but I just had to . . . (Fill in any lame excuse you want here, none of them excuse the fact you have now held us up from our personal life). Providers work an 11-12 hour day, with no breaks from open to close. We cannot leave your child to go out to lunch like you leave your desk. We are not allowed to even smoke in our own back yard, so no smoke breaks. For you to make us work an even longer day so that you can stop at home to change clothes and put dinner in the crock pot is rude and disrespectful.
5. "He had a fever this morning, but it's just because of . . ." We don't care what you self-diagnosed at home with your girlfriends

and WebMD. It could be teething, and it could also be the plague. You do not bring your child to daycare with a temp.

6. "He threw up last night but he has been fine this morning." OK, here's your sign. Besides the fact your child's stomach is empty this morning, the 24 hour rule doesn't say 24 hours unless he looks fine. The minute we feed him breakfast and he hurls all over our floor, we are going to want to make you come and clean it up.

7. "He's had 24 hours of antibiotics" This statement should only be used if it is true. If we sent your child home at noon yesterday and you are on our step at 7AM you are boldface lying to us and it is insulting. It takes at least an hour to go to the doctor and another hour to go to the pharmacy, get the meds, go home and take them. So at the very most your child has had 17 hours, in which time you crammed 3 doses and called it a day. Three doses does not equal 24 hours, so quit it with the scammer math.

8. "Her fever broke this morning, so we went ahead and came." What part of 24 hours is so complicated? Your child must be fever free and medication free for 24 hours. So if you gave your child Tylenol at 8 PM the 24 hours starts at midnight when the Tylenol wears off, and your child's temp has to stay down for a full 24 hours without any additional doses.

9. "Our doctor tells me everyone has already been exposed." Come now, you are an intelligent adult. Surely you get that multiple exposures means an increased risk of infection.

10. "I don't know why you are sending my child home when I know little Johnny had a cough last week." You may know little Johnny had a cough. Little Johnny may have asthma or allergies which are not contagious. He may also have been fever free while your child has 101* temp. Unfortunately because of HIPPA we can't argue any of that with you and we shouldn't have to.

11. "The outfit she has on is brand new. Could you try to keep it clean?" Nope; we can't. Don't bring your child in anything she can't play, eat and paint in. Childcare is not the place for white, new or expensive clothes or shoes.

12. "He just refuses to wear a coat." Who's in charge here, you or the 30 pound tyrant? Put a coat and shoes on your child whether you think it is cold or not when the temp outside is under 60*,

period. Flip flops are not OK for any child in 30* weather, even if you have them on.
13. "We know toys aren't allowed, but he just had to bring it." No he didn't have to bring a gun with little bullets that kids can choke on and everyone will fight over.
14. "I figured it would be fine to bring the check by tomorrow." If you went to get your paycheck and your boss said that to you, would you be happy?"
15. "Suzy said you didn't give her lunch today." Seriously? Yes we tell little children they have to go hungry. Perhaps little Suzy refused lunch because it was meatloaf and not Burger King.
16. "Our child doesn't have to nap at home." Probably your child doesn't have to mind or clean up after himself at home either. Here we rest every day, because your children (and obviously you) don't understand how important sleep is to growing bones and brain development.
17. "He only misbehaves when he's bored." I call B.S. on this one. Children aren't mean because they are bored. They don't bite hit or kick just because there's nothing else to do. In addition your child is going to be bored a lot in their life, and being a brat will never be a good alternative.
18. "She never does that at home." This one usually involves bullying, taking toys or being mean to others. Guess what? Your child doesn't have any reason to do that at home, because she is in her domain, with her toys and probably no other kids to bully. So that comment is not only irrelevant, it is idiotic.
19. "I am working late tonight, so I won't be able to get here until . . . ." Your scheduled pick-up time is what you contracted for. You do not have the right to change it whenever you feel like it without consulting us. You need to ask ahead of time and be fine with being told no, just like you would expect your boss to ask you ahead of time if you could work late.
20. "I forgot to get diapers, so hopefully you can make the ones in her bag last the day." No, hopefully you have time to hit Safeway before work and bring them to me. We won't make your child sit in urine until you come back.
21. "As smart as my child is, and at the level they are at they need to be learning more." Are you implying our children are the dull

crayons in the box? Or are you implying your child is the super special one and we should short-change everyone else?

There are many more offensive and idiotic comments and questions, but you get the drift. Think before you open your mouth. Don't imply we don't care about our job, don't act like not paying us is no big deal and don't make excuses for your bad behavior or your child's.

Addressing Concerns about Care

Along the way there will be times you have concerns you feel like bringing to your provider's attention. This is normal and I encourage open communication. There is such a thing as too much interference, however. You don't want to lose a great provider simply because you feel the need to micromanage every single thing she does with your child.

When you start to feel there is a problem with your childcare, the first step to take is to evaluate how serious the issue is, and what impact it has on your child. You will notice I did not ask what impact the issue has on you. You see, there is a perception that we are here somehow to make your life easier. Take for example the parent that demands that their child's nap be taken away so that they can get him to go to bed at 6PM with no argument. At naptime their child is tired, and by the time the parents pick up he is exhausted and overstimulated. He is more likely to misbehave, less likely to eat well or want to play outside and above all he is missing out on the rest time needed to regenerate his energy and his physical body. Our job is to make sure he gets the rest he needs when he needs it, not to deprive him of sleep in order to force compliance for mom and dad. In fact, most states have regulations that require a rest time and waking a child who is sleeping before they are ready is considered denial of critical care. In this particular case the issue is not about the child, it is about convenience for the parents.

The second question to consider is whether or not you have a basis for worry. Let's say for example, that your concern is that your child will be knocked down by an older child and will be hurt. You should evaluate whether or not your child has been knocked down before, or if other children in care have been hurt the same way. You should also decide how much comfort you have that your provider is careful about supervising your child. You should look at their track record. If their daycare has not had a serious injury in 20 years, they have proven to be trustworthy and have earned the right to be trusted.

The next step is to evaluate if this is a need or want issue. What I mean is, is there something your child needs that they are not getting, or is it something they want but can be fine without? This is where children who scream to be held all day usually fit. You may feel the need to pick your child up every time they cry. Your provider may be fine with letting them fuss for a while in order to teach them to self-soothe. Your provider is not wrong and your child will not be harmed by being allowed to cry for a reasonable period of time (longer than 5 seconds) without being picked up or even responded to.

Sometimes the issue is not with the provider. Here are some examples of issues which cannot be controlled or corrected by a provider.

1. You may not care for another child in the daycare. You may feel they are a bad influence on your child. There are always going to be children in your child's class or Girl Scout troop you don't feel are appropriate. You cannot banish them all. It is your job to teach your child that even though Johnny cusses it is not OK. There may be a parent who feels your child is the unworthy one. We don't terminate care simply because another parent takes exception to a child. The same applies when you dislike another parent. We cannot give a family notice because you object to the fact mom smokes or has body odor.
2. We cannot force other children to like your child or play with them. If your daughter wants to play Babies all the time, the other children in care may not want to join her. Your child may come home and tell you no-one likes her. It is important to explain to your child that making friends will take work and that she will need to play what the other children are playing sometimes, or let someone else be in charge. You will also need to talk about how she acts with other children. Your child is learning how to make friends, and she may think that talking to

them like her big brothers talk to each other is normal, and the other child involved may not want to be called a dummy.
3. We are here to be your child's supervisor, not his best friend. There will be days your child will tell you we don't like them, that we are mean to them and that we pick on them. Should you sympathize without any evidence you will undermine our ability to teach your child respect, empathy and good behavior. It is crucial you encourage your child to understand that we can tell them no and still love them.

The way to determine when to talk with your provider is to ask the following questions of yourself before asking for a sit-down:

1. In thirty words or less, sum up the issue.
2. How does this issue affect my child in a negative way?
3. What do I feel is a practical solution to the program that does not involve my child being treated differently from any of the others?
4. What are ways I can help my child deal with or recover from this adversity?
5. Have we contributed to the problem?
6. Is this issue a safety or health concern?
7. Am I willing to lose my childcare if my provider will not change their policy?

It is always easier to use an example for these things, so here is a good one. The Jones family comes in complaining that they are concerned that their daughter Jayden doesn't want to come to daycare anymore. They feel she is not receiving the attention she needs and is feeling unloved. Here is the breakdown of the questions as asked:

1. To sum it up, Jayden has told them no-one pays attention to her and she doesn't want to come anymore.
2. Jayden may be feeling left out or lonely.
3. Jayden was asked by her parents what would make her feel better, and replied that she wanted to bring her dolls from home and to not have to take naps.
4. The parents can help by explaining that toys have to stay home so that they don't get broken or lost. They can also explain that

simply because Jayden has to take a nap it does not mean anyone hates her. Naps are necessary. The parents can also have Jayden nap on the weekends to keep a consistent schedule.
5. Jayden's parents have unknowingly contributed to the program by allowing her to bring toys to daycare that were then taken away because they are not allowed, which was in the handbook. They also tried to instruct the provider to let Jayden stay up for rest time, even though they knew what the daycare nap policy was. This gave Jayden the indication her parents could make the rules at daycare, and change them for her if she told them she was unhappy.
6. Neither one of these issues is a safety or health concern.
7. These issues should never have come to the provider. To risk alienating a provider simply because they won't let a child run their household is foolish.

Here is another example:

Tommy Miller tells his parents he does not want to go to daycare. He cries all the way there and clings to mom. When asked he cannot give a reason why he does not want to go. He seems to be fine on certain days, but is awful on Monday and Wednesday. Let's go through the questionnaire.

1. The issue is that Tommy seems to be afraid to go to daycare on certain days.
2. Tommy may be being hurt or mistreated
3. When he was asked what would make him feel better, Tommy asked to go to a new daycare where Johnny couldn't go. He then told his parents Johnny pinched him and hit him with toys. Johnny is a bigger child in his class.
4. Tommy's parents can let the provider know what is going on. They can help Tommy to learn to tell the teacher whenever Johnny hurts or scares him. They can teach him to play with other kids and stay away from Johnny. They can teach him to yell "NO, STOP" any time he is being hurt.
5. Tommy's parents have not contributed to this problem. They are a big part of the solution.

6. By working with Johnny on being kind, and keeping the boys apart while supervising them, this can end up being a relationship building problem.

Many times children have a hard time verbalizing what the problem is, so they simplify it by saying no-one loves them or everyone is mean. It is important to get specific examples of what bothers them before going to your provider, because without a specific problem there is very little that can be done.

When you have had a chance to figure out what the problem is and are ready to go and see your provider, make sure to call during a non-hectic time of the day and ask when would be a good time to sit down and talk. Don't make it sound like an emergency by making grand statements about urgent issues that need addressed. Obviously there are issues or you wouldn't be calling. Do not expect her to be able to make time to meet the same day you call, any more than you could drop everything for a meeting with one of your clients. Do not ever ask if you can bring your child with, it is not appropriate. When a parent brings a child to a meeting, they are often tempted to use their child to manipulate getting their way by having the child ask for something the parent knows they cannot have, hoping the provider will say yes and knowing if she doesn't they get to be the sympathetic good guy and make the provider out to be the mean one. Parents also count on the fact that a provider will temper what they say in front of a child, so they can get away with inappropriate comments without being called out.

When talking with your provider about the issues at hand there are ways to get the most from the conversation. These guidelines apply.

1. Ultimatums never result in happy endings. Telling your provider if she doesn't stop letting your child sleep for two hours you will find other daycare is a statement that should only be made if you already have other daycare on hold.
2. Be careful about making grand statements or exaggerating. Don't comment that your child was crying for an hour if it was only 15 minutes. Don't use words like "always" or "never"

3. Never send a message or instructions with your child. Even if your child comes in and tells us you gave them permission not to take a nap, we're still going to give them one, and they are going to be frustrated for no reason.
4. Remember that you are emotionally attached to your child and being objective is next to impossible. Remain calm and polite. Take turns speaking with your provider. Listen while she talks and do not interrupt. Make sure you are actually listening, and not just discounting everything being said.
5. Let your provider know how you plan to help with the changes you want her to make. If you want your child to have more books to read, then be willing to bring books for the daycare. If you want your child to have more juice than your provider serves, be willing to bring juice for the entire group.
6. Do not play the "I pay your salary" or "I am the parent" card. You have to remember that if you actually paid our salary, you would also pay our social security, unemployment and benefits. In addition although we are well aware you are the parent, the moment you leave your child with us and go to work, you hand over all decision making to us, because we are the ones responsible for anything that happens while your child is in our care.
7. Lastly, remember that you cannot give us permission to break the rules. If licensing tells us no blankets in the crib, you cannot give us permission to violate those regulations. If the food program tells us we have to give your child milk with every meal, we cannot give them juice simply because you prefer it.

So to sum it all up, come to us with an actual problem and a practical solution. Otherwise remember you have all of your hours with your child to take care of issues as well.

Discipline—The United Front

Raising a child is a long term effort. It is important not to skip any steps because you cannot get the right end result without putting in the required time and work.

One of the hardest jobs we have as a parent is discipline. It is painful to be the bad guy who has to tell your child no. It can be exhausting to deal with the persistent tantrums and whining, and sometimes the urge is just to give in so that you can have a few seconds of peaceful silence. Each time you give in it gets easier to say yes to avoid conflict.

For most parents, watching someone else make your child unhappy causes an inner rage to come out. You immediately want to take over and comfort your child while they are in the middle of being taught a lesson that needs learning.

For childcare providers discipline is even more taxing. We have far more limitations than parents do when it comes to consequences. We cannot use any form of corporal punishment. We cannot withhold food or rest. We cannot use any form of punishment which may be construed as humiliating. We cannot separate or ostracize a child to make a point.

Thankfully the very best discipline comes from applying natural consequences. It is about teaching a child that A+B=C. For example, when we hit our friend then they don't want to play with us anymore. When we refuse to eat our lunch then we get to have a sandwich for snack instead of a cookie. When we throw a toy the toy goes away.

What becomes difficult is when parents are not consistent with discipline at home and all of the burden falls on the provider during the day to teach those valuable life lessons. In order to get the best result here are some ways that you can work with your provider.

1. It is never a good idea to let a child dictate the terms of their day. Make your morning hassle free by laying everything out at night. There should be no bribery to get your child through the daycare doors.
2. Make sure your child comes to care well rested. Children who are tired have a hard time coping socially and it can lead to aggression. Give your child healthy foods in the morning, not sugary garbage that will have your child bouncing off the walls and then crashing an hour afterwards.
3. Many parents don't realize how important it is to send your child to daycare in appropriate clothing. Short skirts and belly shirts are not ok. Sending your child in expensive clothes and telling them to stay clean will make it hard for your child to participate. Clothes that are not appropriate for the weather can cause your child to feel punished because they cannot go outside.
4. When you arrive at daycare to find your child being disciplined, stay out of it. Do not allow your child to run from the provider to you in an effort to avoid consequences. Take the time to have your child finish their time-out or consequences.
5. Never undermine your provider's authority in front of your child. If you have questions call the provider later. Remember your child is going to give you their version of the event.
6. When you ask your child why they were disciplined, do not accept "I don't know" for an answer. Ask your child if they understand why what they did was wrong and let them know that you and their provider love them, but that there are rules for everyone.
7. Never baby or reward your child after being disciplined because you feel bad. By giving your child a toy or treat right after being in trouble you are sending a mixed message which prevents them from learning their lesson. It is OK and even expected for your child to feel badly after getting in trouble. It is the feeling badly that leads to remembering the next time.

The biggest piece of advice about discipline is this. No provider wants to pick on or be mean to your child. No matter how cute you think their behavior is, if it is not allowed in daycare you should not encourage it. Your child may love karate chopping at your house, and may not understand that your house is the only place it is allowed.

OH THAT PESKY PAPERWORK—
WHAT TO EXPECT IN A CONTRACT

Depending on what kind of childcare you decide to go with, there should be paperwork involved. It is easier to make a table which shows what kind of paperwork you should expect to have to supply. There is also a certain amount of paperwork you can expect to receive from your provider. You will find a table at the end of this chapter which tells you which forms can be expected with each type of care.

Here are some of the common forms:

CHILD INTAKE / CHILD ENROLLMENT FORM: This form is the place where all your basic information goes. It should contain both parents work information, phone numbers for home, work and cell phones. It should have information about your child to include their doctor and dentist, their date of birth and any pertinent information such as medical conditions, allergies and things the provider needs to know to give the best care to your child.

EMERGENCY MEDICAL AUTHORIZATION: This form is to be used if your child is hurt or ill and your provider has to secure medical care for them. This form will contain your child's data, as well as information on both parents. It will list the child's pediatrician and dentist, as well as what hospital you prefer your child be transported to, but please be aware they will go to the closest hospital in a life or death emergency. Basically, with this form you are giving your provider permission to authorize tests, surgeries and treatments to make your child better. This form will also contain your insurance information and a paragraph where you acknowledge you are responsible for the payment for medical care. It is crucial that you update this for any time information on it becomes outdated. If you change jobs and your insurance changes, it is not fair to your provider to have to pay for your child's visit to the ER simply because you forgot to let her know. You need to complete this for fully and as neatly as possible so it can be read by the hospital staff. You should also include a typed letter outlining any special medical information the hospital may need, such as a refusal of blood products for religious reasons. This letter has to be notarized and signed to be legal.

FINANCIAL AGREEMENT: Lays out the terms of payment. It should include what your weekly rate is, and when payment is due each week. It should also state what the charges are for late payments, picking up your child late, going over your allotted hours each week and if there are fees for returned checks in case that should ever be an issue. It will have a paragraph that covers what happens if you should leave without 2 week's notice and what collection costs will be if they ever have to collect from you in court. All of these things are standard.

TRASPORTATION FORM: This is so that you can give permission for walks to the park, riding in a car to the zoo, or a trip by bus to the fair. There should be one in your child's file all the time for transportation to school and back. For field trips most states require that you sign a separate slip each time your child goes somewhere. The slip should tell where your child is going, departure and arrival times and how they will be getting there (bus, car, walk etc . . .).

FOOD PROGRAM FORMS: These forms are very different from state to state and from center to in-home. They will ask for your household income, do not be alarmed. The federal food program pays a higher allowance for children who are low income. Please understand that if you refuse to disclose this information your provider cannot be reimbursed for your children and may have to charge you instead.

PHOTOGRAPH RELEASE: This gives permission for the daycare to use your child's photos or video likeness on their website, brochures etc . . . For your child's safety you should insist that your child's last name never be on the literature, only their last initial.

MEDICATION AUTHORIZATION: This form covers a lot. Did you know that sunscreen and bottom balm are considered medication by the daycare regulations? Yes, that is right. Your provider is supposed to get written permission before putting Balmex on your child's bottom. We have to have permission for Tylenol, bug repellant, Neosporin and everything else. Even lotion is considered a medication. Your provider must keep track of every time she gives your child a pill or liquid and every time she applies something to their skin.

IMMUNIZATION FORMS: Every daycare is required to keep current copies of your child's immunizations to show that they are up to date for the department of public health. They are also required to have a physical for your child every 1-2 years, depending on the state.

PARENT HANDBOOK ACKNOWLEGEMENT: Don't gloss this one over. This handbook is the rules by which you must now live. It will tell you all of the rules and policies of the daycare. It will also tell you what they have to offer your family and what their expectations are from you. This document is legal and binding. You cannot claim you didn't know about the policies if you sign that you have read the handbook. Make sure you ask any questions you have before you sign. If they promise you something verbally make sure they note it in the handbook or on an addendum if it contradicts what the handbook says.

PAYMENT AUTHORIZATION FORM: Some centers have the ability to take credit cards or auto-draft your account. If they are going to do this on the same day every month without getting your consent each month, you should sign an auto-draft form which tells the day of the month and the card or account information which will be used, as well as the amount. You then sign consent for this to be done every month.

If you choose to hire someone in your home, the paperwork is very different. In that case, here are the forms you will encounter, and what they are for.

W-2's: These are to help you deduct taxes from your employee's paycheck. You must have these on file for both federal and state taxes.

You can download these forms from the IRS website and your state department of revenue website as well.

APPLICATION: You should never hire anyone without one of these. You need to evaluate how they have done in the past. If they have not kept a job more than 6 months in 6 years, how can you expect them to stay with you? Don't expect to be the one magical employer they will stay with. And if they have some big story about every place they have ever worked and why they were in the right when they got fired or quit, refer back to the warning I gave you about people whose lives are full of drama.

AUTHORIZATION FOR MEDICAL CARE: Since your nanny will probably be handling some of your child's non-emergency medical visits, such as physicals and check-ups for ear infections, this for covers any kind of medical care, not just life and death emergencies. Once again, all of your insurance information should be on here, as well as the names and contact information for doctor and dentist. You should attach photocopies of your driver's license and insurance cards so that she has them if needed for your child's file at the doctor's office.

JOB DESCRIPTION: The duties you want your nanny to perform need to be laid out in plain English on paper, so that there is no question that you have let them know what you expect. It should include the daily schedule they are to follow, the jobs which need done each day of the week and the general description of those tasks, such as "Dress the children in clean clothes which are appropriate for the weather." This job description can have a weekly calendar included which show tasks such as doing a load of the children's laundry Mon and Wed and changing their bedding on Fri.

BACKGROUND CHECK RELEASE: You will need this after interview 2, so that you can run a background check on each candidate is a viable option.

EMPLOYMENT CONTRACT: This is the paperwork which lays out the hourly pay or weekly salary, as well as any benefits such as room and board, car, insurance etc . . . This employment contract should also include training required and who will pay for it. In addition it should include information about how long a new employee is on probation. An employee handbook which covers dress code, absences and tardiness, appropriate behavior and other codes of conduct is a great idea to include in the contract. The more that you specify what the job entails, the less likely you are to have problems later on with an employee who wants more money because they claim the job is harder than they thought it was going to be.

There can be so many different kinds of forms that you can use. Many centers now have infant forms which tell how your baby ate and slept and you can find them on the web for your nanny to use as well. There are incident reports for when a child gets injured and discipline reports for when a child misbehaves.

Make sure you fill out all of your forms neatly and completely. Also make sure that when your information changes you notify your childcare provider so that the information in your files can be updated. It can mean a tragedy if something happens to a child and the phone numbers for the parents have changed and no-one has been informed. Give as many numbers for family and friends who can find you in an emergency. Make sure you put a work number down for where you work, don't just put your cell phone down for everything. Your provider won't call your boss on a whim.

Walk away from providers who do not have paperwork for you to fill out. This means they are not keeping records of the children they care for, which is against state and federal regulations. It also means they will not have what they need should something happen like a house fire or medical emergency. Insist on seeing the forms they require before you sign up.

In addition, please remember that all of the paperwork you sign is legal documents. Don't sign something you cannot comply with later.

A Back-up Plan for Sick Days

Imagine having 12 kids. OK, maybe that is too big of a stretch for the average person. So now imagine you have four. Now imagine they are 4, 3, 2 and 6 months of age. Already we can see you're starting to sweat. Now they are all four sick with terrible colds and you are running back and forth with Tylenol, bulb syringes, juice, formula and Pedialyte. The baby begins vomiting from the mucus he is swallowing and you begin to think you will never get through this day.

It is at this point your boss taps you on the shoulder and reminds you that you are an insurance agent safe at work. You have one child in daycare, no big deal.

We really weren't joking about the 12 kids. A group C licensed daycare home in Iowa is allowed 12 full time, 2 part-time and 2 school aged children. That means that on the average day the two co-providers on this license are responsible for 16 kids. Which even when they are well is a handful.

In daycare you are bound to get sick kids occasionally. My helper and I try really hard not to make parents come and get their child for no reason. Our illness policy is pretty simple. If your child has a fever over 101*, is vomiting or has explosive diarrhea, we just don't feel he is well enough to come to daycare. Sounds pretty reasonable right? Guess again . . . .

> *We are crazy about baby Josh. At 8 months of age and 23 pounds he is a happy little bowl of Jell-O. Always getting into everything and just about ready to walk, he lights up our morning. His mom on the other hand, sends lightning bolts of fury up our backsides.*

Co-Parenting Strangers

Mona is one of those moms we were talking about with the one sided equation. Not only does she only see her side of the argument, she is amazed when you don't.

Monday is always a hectic day. With the seasons changing there are a few runny noses here and there. So when Josh came with a runny nose we weren't surprised. We were a little worried that he took 2 three hour naps. We chalked it up to the rainy day outside. On Tuesday, however, we knew.

Mona brought Josh through the door at 7 AM with his shirt soaking wet and smelling like vomit. Not like spit-up from formula he had just had but stomach bile and rotten milk. I immediately began the intervention. "It looks like he's thrown up" I commented. "Has he been sick this morning?"

"I think he just swallowed some mucus." Mona replied "I cleaned his nose out with a bulb syringe that's in his bag, but I didn't have a change of clothes in the car. If he gets too bad just let me know" I nodded and went off to find clean clothes and a soapy rag as she headed out the door.

All day long Josh spit back up everything we fed him. We syringed and wiped and changed his clothes three times. We kept letting mom know that he wasn't keeping food down, and she kept promising to call the doctor and get him in. When she picked him up at 4:30 I let her know that she would need to keep him upright and not on his back, and that she would need to get a doctor's appointment as soon as possible. I sent them out the door expecting that I would not see Josh again on Wednesday.

6:40 A.M. on Wednesday there they were on my doorstep before I was even open for the day. Mona smiled as she breezed in with baby Josh on her arm, green rivers of snot running down to his chin. "I totally forgot to tell you I had an early meeting this morning" she gushed happily. "I'll call you as soon as it's over to see if I need to come and get him."

Now I was getting upset. "Mona, I can't keep him if he continues to throw everything up. I'm worried he'll get dehydrated or choke when we're turned away with another child."

"Well dad is still out of town and I cannot miss this meeting. It's for my new promotion. Besides, he's been doing much better. He hasn't thrown up at all this morning and we've been up for an hour. I'll call you as soon as it's over." She sped out the door before I could think of how to tell her no. And right then Josh threw up what looked like oatmeal and bananas all over my shirt.

By noon Jessica and I were fed up. Josh had thrown up breakfast, morning snack and the Pedialyte we gave him for lunch. I informed Jessica it was her turn to call. God forbid I open my mouth or I was going to be rude. I could only hear one side of the conversation but it was enough to know it wasn't going well. "She said she has to go find her manager and she'll call us back." was Jess's comment as she went to put mats out for naptime.

An hour later still no call. Jess called again. This time I could hear the argument. "We really need for you to come and get him." A pause and then "Mona he hasn't held anything down for us in 2 days . . ." another pause "He's just too sick to be here." I watched as Jess's eyes glassed over and her face took on that red tint it gets when she is about to nuke someone. Then all of a sudden she hung up.

"She said her manager is in a meeting and she can't get to her right now and she'll call us back. Then she hung up on me"

I knew my blood pressure was probably through the roof by now. This wasn't a person whose business would close if she went home. Her company had several hundred employees just in her division alone. I knew she had vacation and sick time available because she had planned to take 2 weeks off in a month and had made the comment she was glad she had saved her sick days. I made the comment to Jess that I did not think we would see Mona before *quitting time no matter how many times we called. We continued to keep Josh as comfortable as possible and waited.*

When Josh's normal pick up time of 4:30 PM came and went I grew more and more angry. Finally at 5:30, Mona strolled through the door with a "Hey, Mama how's your day?"

"My day has been a lot better than your little one's has. Did you have trouble getting off work on time?" I wasn't actually asking to be polite, but I shouldn't have asked at all because the answer just pi**^d me right off.

"No, I stayed and got some extra work done because the doctor can't see him until 6. I figured since I would have to come out here to get to the doctor's I would just wait until it was time to take him."

I handed her the baby bag and made my first definitive statement. "He last threw up at 3:30, so he won't be able to come back tomorrow because he has to be 24 hours free from vomiting." Pretty clear statement, right?

"Well, we'll go see what the doctor has to say . . . . I'll call you later." She strolled to her truck and had the nerve to wave as she backed out of the drive. So much for clear statements.

At that point I needed a break from everyone. I loaded up our daughter and told my husband that if Mona called I expected him to hold firm, and under no circumstances allow her to plan on bringing her child to daycare the next day. Mick assured me he could handle it. I made it halfway to the grocery store and the cell phone rang.

"She's already calling." I resisted the urge to laugh. "She's says that Dr. Waylan told her it's just a cold and he's fine to return to daycare. I told her can't come back until Friday and she insisted she needs to speak with you because she knows other kids have

come sick and she doesn't see why she should have to miss a day of work for a cold."

The urge to laugh was replaced with the urge to jump from a tall building. "I told her you would call her back but that you would have the same answer for her I did. Then she informed me she was biting her tongue and hung up."

It was two hours later when I decided I was ready to call Mona back. I got voice mail. I politely informed her digital receptionist that although I just love Josh, I cannot give him the care and attention he needs when he is that miserable. So as long as he didn't throw up on Thursday at home he would be welcome back on Friday. I let her know I was out and therefore she would not be able to call me back and hung up.

Josh was back on Friday, still sick. My daughter and I spent our weekend with Mucus running down our throat until we were throwing up. Mona got her 30 day notice on Monday. The next week we had 5 more children become ill with what was diagnosed as RSV, all because one woman didn't want to use a vacation day.

Getting up to find your child ill on a day when you have to work is a major problem for most parents. Some don't have sick time or vacation because they are hourly employees. Some parents work by themselves and if they take the day off there is no-one to keep the business open. Then there are some who just don't want to deal with a sick child. This is one area however, where providers will put their foot down. Continue making our family and other clients ill, and you will be gone.

There are ways you can avoid Mona's fate. Every parent should have a plan for sick days. If your child is in daycare, they will become ill more often than a child who is at home. Even super-vigilant providers and centers can't keep germs from spreading 100% of the time. A great deal of childhood illnesses like chicken pox, are contagious before you even know your child has them, making it impossible to keep them from spreading.

Co-Parenting Strangers

Discuss with your husband how you will handle days when your child is ill. If one of you has a more flexible job, that parent can cover sick days most of the time. If only one of you has vacation and sick days you really have no choice.

If you have grandparents or aunts and uncles who stay home, ask them if they would be willing to pick your child up if you can't in the event he becomes ill. You will have to make sure they are listed on the forms you give your provider. You will also need to have a plan for how they will get a car seat from you if they don't have one.

Save some of your days off for these emergencies. If you use all of your days off for fun and vacation you will be more likely to try and take your child to daycare sick because you don't want to lose the income.

Don't cry wolf: If you don't feel like going to work, don't tell your boss your child is ill. You don't want to get in trouble when your child actually is ill for missing too much work. Murphy's Law says that if you play hooky today with the excuse of a sick child, they will come down with the crud tomorrow.

It is a cardinal sin to take your child to daycare when you know for a fact they are ill. If you have to give them Tylenol to break a fever, keep them home. If you are dosing them with cold medicine in order to drop them off, understand that it will wear off. You may get a half a day of work out of it but your provider will remember and you will not get any flexibility in the future.

Be honest with your provider if you think your child is becoming ill. Calling your provider and letting them know that your child has a runny nose and you think it is teething but you can't be sure will go much further than giving them Benadryl and hoping the problem will go away.

This doesn't mean that even if your child has a runny nose you are homebound. It simply requires common sense on your part. Understanding some of the symptoms providers are serious about can help you avoid problems.

1. Many parents immediately want to blame a fever on teething. Although teething can sometimes cause a very low grade fever, if your child has a fever of 101* or higher, it needs to be investigated because it is far more likely to be illness.

2. Vomiting is another rough one. Usually a provider will wait until your child vomits a second time before requiring you come and get them. This ensures it isn't from playing too hard, crying excessively etc . . . There is no way to determine the cause without a doctor.

3. Another big issue parents get upset about is having to pick their child up for diarrhea. It is important to talk to your provider about any medicines your child may take that could cause diarrhea so that she will know your child is having a reaction as opposed to an illness. If your child has more than 2 watery stools in 2 hours and they are not on medication, they should not go to daycare.

4. Other reasons a child will be sent home include an unexplained rash, unidentifiable sores or bumps, unusual behavior such as listlessness or indications of dehydration. These are all conditions that require a doctor's note before returning to care.

Childcare providers receive these guidelines from the State regulatory agency and from their local childcare training offices. They don't enforce them to be mean or to single anyone out. If you are concerned your child is being sent home far too often and for no good reason, here are some questions to ask about an illness policy.

1. If my child has an illness that is not contagious, such as an ear infection, will they be able to attend childcare? Do I need a doctor's note?
2. If I bring a copy of the list of side effects for my child's medication and diarrhea is on it, will they be allowed to stay as long as they have no other symptoms?
3. If my child has a common cold, at what point will he need to be picked up? (some providers will tell you if his mucus is green instead of clear, some draw the line at vomiting)

Don't be angry at a provider who demands a note from the doctor stating that your child's illness is not contagious. Providers have had a long history of bad luck with parents who call and say "the doctor said . . ." and then feed them a load of bologna. Providers have to worry about the greater good. Sending one child home to keep ten healthy is the responsible thing to do.

Always obey the 24 hour rule. An illness can be contagious for up to 24 hours after vomiting, diarrhea and fever disappear. We rely on parents to be honest about when a child stops throwing up or when their fever breaks without the help of Tylenol. If your child's fever breaks at nine at night, seven the next morning is not soon enough to put your child in a room with other children.

After your child is feeling better and you plan on returning to daycare it is important to sanitize things that will be going with your child. The following are a list of items and how to make sure they aren't germ carriers.

   A. Blankets, car seat covers and jackets should be washed and dried in a hot dryer
   B. Stuffed animals should be placed in the dryer on high heat for one hour
   C. Bottles and pacifiers should be washed in a dishwasher with heated dry or rinsed with bleach water if washed in the sink.
   D. Hard toys and rattles should be sprayed with 10% bleach 90% water solution and then dried or steamed with a high pressure steamer. They can also be washed in the dishwasher with heated dry.
   E. Bulb syringes should be cleaned by sucking up hot water and blowing it out several times, then sucking up hydrogen peroxide and letting it sit for 10 minutes before blowing it out. Then do hot water one more time to rinse.
   F. Thermometers should be wiped with an alcohol wipe.
   G. Wipe down the plastic on the car carrier with hand sanitizer or alcohol.

These are great practices for any time your child is ill. They take about 2 hours which is time well spent.

When you take your child to the doctor, write down exactly what the name is for what your child has. Ask the following questions so that you are educated and can talk with your provider.

1. Is this contagious?
2. How is it spread?
3. How long will my child be sick?
4. When can my child return to daycare without infecting others?

Take your pediatrician's advice seriously. Doctor's don't want to tell parents they have to miss work so if they tell you your child should stay home they are serious about it.

Be sure when you do return to childcare you bring your child's medicine in the original container, with their name and the instructions on it. This is the law in most states. In addition, if your doctor wants your child on an over the counter medicine—have him write instructions for your childcare provider. Otherwise she is breaking the law giving non-prescribed medicine to your child.

As long as you have a strong plan for your child's sick days and are receptive to working with your provider to keep all of the children in her care safe, she will appreciate your efforts and work with you as much as she can. Just remember how it feels when you are caring for one sick child and appreciate that adding 11 more would be impossible for even a saint.

Save the Drama for Your Mama

As childcare providers we see drama all day long. There are a lot of times we wish the world would just stay outside and leave the kids inside with us. You see we really enjoy our job when we can do it without nonsense coming through our door.

We understand that sometimes things happen. Occasionally a parent is going to run late. There will be times things will go wrong.

There are other times when we realize a client thrives on drama. This means that sooner or later their drama is going to infect our business, our home and our family life. Here are some of the ways drama mamas can rock our world.

1. "Speed Racer" is always running late. During the drop off routine this mom practically rips their child's arms out of socket getting the coat off. She is short and angry with her child and has no time for kisses or talk. At the pick-up end this mom is irritated that no-one had ESP and got her child's shoes and hat on before she even arrived.
2. "Martyr Mary" likes to remind you what a terrible hardship it is to comply with any request. She has to let you know how impossible it is to find a back-up sitter so that you can have a personal day off. She likes to moan about how much work she couldn't get done because her child had to be home sick. This mom makes you feel like you are burdening her when you ask for a spare t-shirt.
3. "Stacker Sally" likes to make little passive aggressive remarks with each little thing that happens and place them all in a mental stack like plates. Child poopy when picked up, one plate. Bottle given 20 minutes late, another plate. Child trips and splits lip,

another plate. And then one day the imaginary stack gets too tall and all of a sudden she is hurling every mistake she thinks you ever made right in your face, usually right in the middle of your busiest time.

4. "Bitters" are the angry couple divorcing. These guys will bad mouth each other every chance they get. They will ask questions that have nothing to do with the children and are simply designed to dig up dirt on their ex. They will blame the ex for being late picking up, being late paying and for the fact their child is sick when they drop them off. They will make ridiculous requests, such as "please don't send any of her good clothes to her dad's house" and "Make sure he doesn't get to pick her up early for his visits". In extreme cases these idiots will try to use us to enforce whatever visitation they feel like bestowing, and they have the nerve to be pissed when we explain to them that we have to turn their child over to "That Bastard" or we could be arrested. They will try to turn us against their ex by regaling us with tales of how neglectful and abusive he is, and how they are the victim just trying to do what is best for the children.

5. "The Boss" is the parent who thinks they are your employer. They want to micromanage what cleaners you use and what books you read. They will even express opinions about families who call them for a reference. Some Bosses make friendly suggestions pretending you have a choice; some just make it clear what needs to happen to make them happy.

6. "Bubbles" is the parent who forgot the paperwork, the diapers, formula and occasionally they forget it is their turn to pick up their child. They will leave you with no supplies, waiting on them to figure out that it is their turn to pick up the little bundle because their spouse has a meeting. Meanwhile they are at home not even wondering why they haven't seen their spouse or their child. These are the parents who will cause the most licensing violations because you will have to refuse to take their child back until you get current shot records and enrollment forms. They will also be the one to bust in on your morning shower because they forgot to tell you they had a 6AM meeting and would be dropping off two hours early!

7. "O.P.P.'s" are the parents who obsess that there is something wrong every moment of the day. They want to know why little Johnny in the corner has a runny nose. They want to make sure your whole family have had pertussis shots and that their princess will never share toys with others. It is the highlight of my day when I get to tell these parents for the first time that their child ate dirt, or even better, boogers. But you had better not run out of soap or hand sanitizer with these parents around or you will be in trouble. On the bright side all you have to do is tell them you heard a sniffle and they will run their child to the Emergency Department, sure it is RSV.
8. "Cleopatra" is the parent that will tell you with a straight face that their child never cries, poops in his pants, hits or bites at home. They never have issues of any kind and their child may possibly be the most genius child on the planet, even when eating his own scab. If anything is going wrong at daycare rest assured it is because of something you are doing wrong. These parents think there is a simple solution. Just don't do anything that would make their child feel like he has to act out.

In addition to the drama created by these different characters, there are some forms of drama that almost every parent causes. These dramatic moments are caused due to bad behaviors from a parent who may be great most of the time. Here are examples of some dramatic moments.

- There is the moment you have to explain to all the parents their child has been exposed to head lice, because another parent knew their older child had it and didn't check the younger one.
- There is the moment you have to take the cookies and soda away from a 3 year old at 7AM because that's what their parent gave them to eat in the car.
- There is the four hours you can't use the bouncy seat (while cleaning it) because a parent laid their child down in a diaper from the night before without changing them, and without telling you so that you could take care of it.
- There are the days you change shirts 5 times because dad forgot to give the baby their acid reflux medicine.

- There are the countless visits to the doctor with your own children after parents medicate theirs and drop them off sick, claiming everything is fine.
- There are the mornings on the phone with the bank checking to see if you are in overdraft because a parent hasn't paid and your bills are automatic.
- There are the evenings apologizing to your child, your PTA, your book group, your college classmates and countless others for being late because yet another parent couldn't make picking up their child on time a priority.

There are so many of these little moments it is impossible to list them all. These are specific examples of why not everyone can handle this job. They are also reasons that you may find us to be less than cordial some days when we meet you at the door. You may not even be the offending parent that day, but you may be the next one through the door and we may have not had a time-out yet. Don't take it personally unless we tell you to.

THE CHILD AND ADULT FOOD PROGRAM

Many providers across the country, as well as a large number of centers participate in the USDA Child and Adult Food Program. This is a program sponsored by the US government which reimburses providers a portion of the cost of the meals they feed the kids provided they meet the following guidelines:

1. Daily records have to be kept which include in and out times for each child, as well as which meals and snacks each child is served. You notice I say served. Providers do have to offer these foods to the kids. The kids choose whether or not to eat them.
2. Milk must be served with all meals. It has to be cow's milk and it has to be 2% for infants under two and 1% for older children. Parents cannot choose to deviate from this option without a doctor's written instructions.
3. Meals must have all 4 food groups, and the kids must be served the USDA recommended portion.
4. Snacks must have a minimum of two different food groups.
5. All foods served must be listed as credible in the CACFP program. We will cover this more in a moment.
6. Meals and snacks must be no less than 2 and no more than 3 hours apart from each other. In other words, you cannot serve breakfast at 8 AM and snack at 9:30 AM: you must wait until after 10:00 so that there are two hours between the two. You also cannot serve breakfast at 7 AM and lunch at 11 AM with no AM snack in between, because there are more than 3 hours between the two meals.
7. Providers on the food program are asked to include food and nutrition topics in their preschool learning activities.

8. While on the food program, the daycare home or center is subject to random inspections, to include observation of meals served and inspection of the kitchen, food storage and food preparation areas. Providers are required to log fridge and freezer temperatures daily.
9. Centers on the food program are required to keep receipts for all food purchased, and to log how much was used for each meal, and how much was disposed of after. They are required to mark every can or package of food when it is opened and dispose of it after the 3rd day in most cases. They must also keep track of where the leftover food goes. This means that someone has to multiply 1.5 ounces of chicken for every 2 year old and have receipts to prove they bought enough. It is a mountain of documentation and it gets audited without notice.
10. Providers have to enter different menus for each infant age group and for children over 12 months. Children over 12 months are required to be on the regular menu even if they do not have enough teeth to eat it, because there is no option for customizing a menu. So on paper it looks like a one year old with no teeth is eating pork chops, when they are actually having pureed chicken.
11. At 12 months providers must begin serving cow's milk to infants. Formula is no longer an option except as a snack. Want an exception? Make an appointment with your pediatrician.
12. Breakfast on the food program is a grain, a fruit and milk. Eggs and hash browns are great, but your provider won't serve them because they won't get reimbursed. They can be paid for a Pop Tart but not for an egg.
13. Bacon is not a meat. Sausage is fine and so is bologna. Celery is only a vegetable if you serve it with another vegetable such as carrots but Doritos are a vegetable all by themselves. The main ingredient is corn, right?
14. Juice has to be 100%. Your provider cannot serve Sunny D or a juice drink. She also cannot water your child's juice down for you, even if it does give your child tummy trouble, and she cannot serve him/her less than the required portion.
15. Every time your provider serves your child supper, or any meal on a federal holiday, there is yet another fun form which she has to fill out and have parents sign if she wants reimbursed.

16. For families with infants, providers must offer to provide formula when they are on the food program. They can choose which brand to offer, and providers will often offer an off (generic) label formula to save money.

These are just a few of the fun facts you need to be aware of when it comes to the food program. There will be a form for you to fill out annually, and the CACFP will send you questionnaires about your income to see if your provider qualifies for a higher reimbursement, because for some reason a bureaucrat decided it costs us more to make lunch for a poor child than a rich one. Please understand that we feel these forms are just as intrusive as you do. We don't compare forms to see which parents make more, or use them to see if you can afford a rate increase. If you don't qualify as low income, then just write "Do not qualify" on the lines and send the form back in. The government does not have a need to know this information unless you are low income, which will mean twice as much reimbursement for your child's meals. We do not have a need to see these forms, so you can seal them in an envelope or mail them directly to the food program.

For those of you who think that your provider is making a killing on the food program bear this in mind. Providers who are on the lower tier get about $.27 for a snack and less than $2 for a meal with 5 food groups in it. For providers who follow the guidelines, the reimbursement only covers about 1/3 to ½ the actual food cost.

In addition to all of the documentation, there are also regulations regarding food storage and kitchen clean-up. There is a specific 4 step dish washing procedure as well as guidelines for what to use to clean and sanitize surfaces.

As a parent there are ways you can make life a little easier on your provider. Understand that it is impossible for us to do breakfast for each child as they come through the door. So if your child is used to instant gratification giving them a small snack before arriving will help your child wait until everyone has arrived and your provider can get breakfast on the table for everyone.

Remember that your provider has to offer your child a variety of healthy food choices. It is not your provider's fault if your child refuses to eat them. If your child is coming home hungry at night it may be because they refuse to eat carrots and meatloaf and are holding out for chicken nuggets and fries. Eating healthy begins and ends at home, so if you are feeding your child sugar cereal and fast food, don't be surprised when they go hungry at daycare. When your child gets hungry enough they will eat. Whatever you do, do not compound the problem by giving them whatever they want to eat right after picking them up. This will cause them to re-adjust their eating schedule so that McDonald's after daycare becomes a late lunch.

Last of all, food allergies are serious business. If your child has an allergy to a food or food group make sure your provider has an up to date care plan signed by your doctor letting her know what to do in case of an exposure. In addition, if there are meds used when your child is exposed you must make sure your daycare has them on hand at all times. Ask your doctor for an extra bottle or epi-pen to leave at daycare, so that there is no risk you will forget it at home. If you do forget, don't be angry at your provider for asking you to go home and get it. We don't like to play the game of odds when it comes to a medical condition. You can risk going without, we cannot.

So, feed your child good food. Make sure we have enough breast milk every day. Make sure you bring us formula before we run out. Understand we can't make your child peanut butter sandwiches every meal and if you want an exception to our rules get a doctor's note for us. Never bring your child through our door with junk food, and never bring junk food in when you come to get them. If you want to bring treats, make them healthy. Most of all, understand how the food program works so that you aren't getting frustrated with us over things we cannot change for you.

Handling Emergencies

Childcare centers and homes have strict guidelines when it comes to being emergency prepared. It may surprise you to know that many providers are less than diligent and some are even downright careless when it comes to planning for disaster.

When you interview providers it is important to ask about emergency planning. There should always be tornado and fire plans posted by every exit so that you can see the evacuation path. There should be a section in the paperwork you fill out that tells you where your child will be taken in the event of an evacuation. There should also be a section letting you know how you will be notified. In the case of our childcare, we have keys to a church up the street, and we have a phone tree in place where two of our parents will call all of the others while we handle caring for the children until they are picked up.

Not only do you want to make sure your provider is having regular drills with the kids, you should also be having drills at home. Make an evacuation plan for your home and practice getting out safely and where you will meet up.

Your provider is required to have smoke detectors in every child occupied room. They are required to have carbon monoxide detectors and fire extinguishers on each floor. In some states providers are required to have a radon test if care is being provided in a basement. If radon levels are high the provider is required to put in a mitigation system.

The list of other safety requirements is about 10 pages. It can be found on your state's website for their regulatory agency. It will include things like outlet protectors in all of the outlets, gates or doors barring entrance to stairways in order to prevent falls and much more.

The most important aspect of all of this is the proper paperwork. Every provider is required to have emergency medical authorization forms for every child. In addition they are required to have contact phone numbers for every parent located by the phone and in the car when transporting any child. It is your responsibility to make sure that your provider always has up to date contact information for you and your spouse. This includes keeping your provider updated when your child's doctor or dentist changes, when there is a change in your child's health such as a new allergy to a medicine, and detailed information every time your child is given any kind of medication. Here is an example of how things can go very wrong:

> *Leslie, a daycare parent of a 4 year old named Kylee. Having started a new job Leslie did not want to miss any work. When Kylee got a cold, Leslie gave her a children's cold medicine in the morning and dropped her off at daycare. She did not want the provider to send her daughter home for being ill so she chose not to say anything.*
>
> *An hour after arriving at care Kylee's temperature rose to 102*. The provider, following the medical plan in her handbook gave Kylee a dose of Tylenol while trying to reach mom. Because she did not know Kylee had already been given medication, she accidentally caused an overdose and permanent liver damage. Had Leslie been forthcoming about the medication she had given, the provider could have used an alternative medication such as ibuprofen, or withheld medication until mom could pick up her child.*

It is critical that parents are honest about any circumstance that could lead to a crisis in childcare. This would include:

- Any injury received at home, such as a fall or blow to the head.
- Any vomiting, fever, diarrhea or dark/discolored urine
- Any medications given for any reason!!!!
- Any persons who may try to see or pick up the child who are not supposed to
- Any extreme changes in behavior or affect while at home

- Any unusual bruises or marks and how and when they occurred
- Any rash, hives or welts
- Any emotional trauma or event affecting your child

Understand we aren't looking for excuses to send your child home. We want to know what is going on so that we can help your child with their needs, and so that we can protect the other children in our care as well. It is always in your best interest to tell us what is going on. If a neighbor child leaves a bruise on your child's back, we don't want to find it and wonder all day where it came from. And if your child is acting out of it and groggy, it helps to know they had a new allergy medicine so that we can watch for negative side effects.

If your child has any kind of medical condition, then you should have an emergency care plan for your provider to instruct her how to respond when your child has an episode. This might include a care plan for a peanut allergy with instructions on when to use the epi-pen. It might also be guidelines for the use of an inhaler for a child with asthma. The plan should have clear directions signed by your child's doctor, and should be reviewed every 6-12 months.

Your provider should have a place for medications and emergency plans. Both should be taken in the car any time your child is transported. They should be kept in a clearly marked container where they can be easily found.

In addition your provider is required to have an adequately stocked first aid kit for the childcare and it should be clearly marked. When you enroll your child ask about the location. Your provider should also have a 72 hour kit for emergencies. A 72 hour kit is a container with enough food, water, diapers etc . . . to care for the daycare children for 72 hours if trapped because of a tornado, blizzard etc . . . This kit should be located in the safe room used during a tornado. It should be checked and restocked every 90 days.

Your provider should have a room she can lock herself in with the children in case of an unwelcome visitor. She should also have 2 or 3 emergency contacts that can come to help with the daycare in case of an emergency. These could be neighbors, parents or family/friends. These individuals should have a background check on file with the state so that they can care for the children should the provider be the one with the emergency. They should know the location of everything needed for care. Here's why:

> *Just like me, my mother still does childcare in her late 60's. She has 8 little ones every day. A few months ago I got a phone call from her. She sounded confused and upset and kept telling me that someone had come into her kitchen and made muffins and gotten all of her knitting out and put it on the table. Something was not right.*
>
> *After calling my back-up provider to come to my home and take over with my co-provider I drove to my mom's house. She was unable to tell me what she had done all day. There were 6 children in her living room, and she could not tell me any of their names. In addition, she did not know where her paperwork was kept or where the contact numbers were posted.*
>
> *I called my 21 year old son to come and take her to the ER. Because I could not find the contact numbers, I had to wait while caring for children I knew nothing about. The older children could tell me the younger one's names but not what kind of formula they took or any other kind of useful information. I prayed not to screw anything up. As each parent arrived I gave them their child and got a number to call them. By the time I got to the hospital I was sure my mom had a stroke, and I was panicking over how to keep both her daycare and mine going until she could recover.*
>
> *As it turned out, my mom had a bad reaction to a painkiller she had gotten after having 3 teeth removed. The drug caused transient global amnesia which mimics a stroke. She was fine 48 hours later, but she will never remember the lost hours that day. Had she not called me to complain about muffins in her kitchen I can't even think about what could have happened? After she was feeling better we went over where all of the paperwork and information was. Two weeks later the drug was taken off the*

> market. It was a fluke that could have resulted in children left without anyone to care for them, had she wandered out the door in her confusion.

Every provider should have plans for Fire, Medical emergency, Tornado or Earthquake, Unwelcome visitor, Severe weather, Power outage, Gas leak and Bomb threat. Emergency numbers for police, fire, poison control and other important numbers such as the gas and electric company should be posted by the phone.

In addition your provider should have a plan for her own unexpected emergencies. You should know how her illness or emergency absences will be handled. Does she have a certain number of sick days built into her contract? Does she have a list of back-up providers or do you need to have your own? If her own child becomes ill, will she close or simply separate her child from the daycare children?

There will be times a child will come to care with a serious and contagious illness. A parent may bring their child to daycare with what they think is a cold. A day later their child may be diagnosed with whooping cough. Some illnesses require the state health department be notified, and this may lead to a letter from the health department being handed out to parents. There is no need to panic when receiving one of these notices. It is important to read and follow the directions in the letter in order to keep everyone healthy and safe.

Remember the goal of childcare is safe happy children. Don't be angry if called to pick up your child because the water is off at your daycare. Proper hand-washing keeps your child from getting sick.

Last of all, save a few PTO days for when disasters happen at daycare. After all, you have to plan for emergencies too. When completing your paperwork for daycare, include as many back-up individuals as you can, so that if you cannot get there to pick up your child there is someone who can. Make sure you let these people know they are on your emergency list.

You are still the number one teacher in your child's life. Have drills at home regularly and do them correctly. Make sure in a fire drill to crawl low to the ground and cover your face with a cloth. In a tornado drill practice getting as quickly as possible to an interior room and teach your child how to back into a corner and cover themselves for protection. In an earthquake drill make sure you are showing your children multiple safe zones, in case they cannot get to a doorway. Teach your child their full name, their address and phone number. Make sure they know your full names. Then teach them about 911. If you and your provider both prepare your child they will be a lot less frightened if and when something happens.

When to Take Action

A child's safety is sacrosanct. If you feel that any child is at risk with a provider then morally you are required to take action, just as you would want someone to step up to protect your child. Here are some guidelines for when to report a provider, when to take your child out of care and when to talk with the provider first.

You should never see your provider raising their hand to your child. It is important to remember that as abhorrent as you may feel it is they have the right to spank their own. I use the word spank, because there is a difference between hitting and spanking. Your provider should not be spanking their child in front of daycare children. They should remove their child to a separate room to discipline. You may not feel comfortable with a provider who spanks their child, but just like you they have the right to their own parenting beliefs. Over the years only a few of my childcare parents have even been aware that I spank my children when necessary. In Iowa the childcare regulations state that a provider will not spank their child in the daycare, and it is grounds for losing your license because it is considered traumatic for the other children to see a child being spanked. I agree with that assessment.

Bumps and bruises are a normal part of growing up. Your child will have bruises on their knees and the front of their legs from falling when learning to walk or running during play. They will have bruises on their elbows and bumps on their forehead. What is not to be expected are bruises on the back, buttocks, around the upper arms or the back of the neck. These are however some of the areas that will tip an expert off to abuse. If bruises appear on these areas ask immediately what happened and watch for signs of dishonesty. Take pictures of the bruises and document, even if you think your provider is telling the truth and it was a fluke accident where your child fell on a toy.

Children are very intelligent and can sense an adult in emotional crisis. They can exaggerate or tell the parent half the story in order to secure undivided attention. They learn early on that being sick or hurt makes them the beloved superstar right away. It is imperative that while listening to your child talk about how they got hurt that parents keep their face and voice neutral, so that the child will relay accurate information.

A great way to know how your provider talks with your child is to sit and listen to your child at play. Get some babies and play daycare with your child. Then watch how they talk to the daycare babies. If they are giving bottles, hugs and kisses all is well. If they are telling the babies to "Shut up the damn screaming" it is time to run to a new daycare. Bear in mind that your child also repeats how you behave during play at daycare. It is a sobering thought that your provider may hear your child calling the baby dolls a little s*#t because you had a moment of crazy brought on by exhaustion.

There is always a period of adjustment in a new childcare. Extreme changes in behavior can be an indication something is wrong. If your child cries and clings to your leg at drop off after 2 weeks, then hide behind the door and wait to see if he stops the moment you are out the door. Or ask your provider to send video footage from her phone so that you can see that everything is going well the moment he can't see you. If your child is playing happily every day when you come to pick them up, then the crocodile tears at drop off don't need to be a large concern. During the separation anxiety phase your child will cry when being handed off to anyone. This period happens between 10 months and almost 2 years and is totally normal.

If your child is still in diapers, frequent diaper rashes are an indication of less than adequate care. Mark your child's diaper with a small mark in an area where it won't be seen. Then pop back in a few hours later and see if it has been changed. If the answer is no, then put another marked diaper on and see if it is still on when you pick up. If your child is sitting in a diaper for 4 or more hours unless the diaper is completely dry you need to terminate care.

If your child becomes ill frequently while in childcare, ask questions about how your provider is sanitizing to prevent transmission. If your child is coming home with fleas or lice constantly it is time to change daycares. You should not see mice, cockroaches or rats in your provider's home, because these pose a serious health risk. Should you find that your daycare home has any kind of infestation it is best to remove your child while it is handled. If the infestation reoccurs it is time to make a permanent change.

Your provider should not be leaving your child with anyone who is not background checked and approved by the state licensing agency to be there as a substitute. If there are different people watching your child every time you show up during the day you should terminate care right away. You are not paying your provider to pay someone else; you are paying her to be with your child.

Your child should never be left alone. If you show up and your provider is walking home from the neighbors while your child is asleep in her house, you should not only withdraw your child but a phone call to the licensing board is required. There has actually been a case in Iowa where a provider was leaving the house while the kids were asleep for nap and going to the grocery store. She was caught when a parent waited around the corner and watched. When she saw the provider leave with no children she called 911. The police could see the kids through the front window and arrested the provider when she returned. The same rule applies if every time you pull in you see children in the front yard with no adult. Even if the front yard has a fence, your child should not be playing in view of traffic or people walking past unless there is an adult right there with them. A back yard with a high fence (over 5 feet) is the absolute best option and even then the provider should have the children in view at all times, even if it is through a patio door or large window. Most states require that an adult be with the children even in the back yard.

You should report your provider immediately if you see or suspect the following:

- Your provider is consuming alcohol during daycare hours, no matter how little
- Your provider is taking medications that alters their mental status, such as narcotics

- Someone is smoking in the daycare home
- There are more children in the daycare home than are allowed on the license
- There is a convicted felon or registered sex offender in the daycare home
- Conditions in the home are unsafe

Sometimes you may have concerns about a daycare home but have no specific reason why. It is always better to err on the side of safety. Here are some warning signs that are less obvious but just as important:

It is not OK for your provider to meet you at the door morning and night and never let you into the home. If they grab the baby from you in the AM and hand him out the door already in his coat every day you should wonder why you cannot go in and get him.

If your daycare does not have an open door policy and the door is always locked there could be a simple explanation. Some providers live in less than desirable neighborhoods. Some providers have children in their care who try to escape out the front door when no-one is looking. There are also providers who want to know exactly who is at the door because a surprise visit from licensing would not go well. This is one of those areas where you need to try and decide if the locked door is for safety or secrecy. If a daycare has a no visit policy during the day, meaning you cannot stop in to see your child they are most likely not following the rules and should be avoided. There is nothing wrong with a sign on the door letting people know they need to have an appointment or that solicitors are not welcome. You should be able to stop in and see your child whenever as long as you are not disrupting nap or asking them to wake your child and then leaving them with a tired cranky little one after 5 minutes. Open door policies are a gift and should not be abused. You should not be popping in every week and making your child miserable because you show up and then leave them there. And you should be in and out in less than 15 minutes, because it disrupts your provider's day to work around you while trying to stick to a schedule. Here's an example:

> Amy was an awesome mom. Her daughter Libby was one and was into everything. When mom was gone, Libby would sit and

play with her toys and laugh at the other kids around her. Mom however, liked to pop in every day and spend an hour holding down our couch making work calls. Unfortunately as soon as she saw mom, Libby became a whiny mess. She would cry to be held. Mom's cell would ring, and instead of putting Libby down and going into another room, she would expect one of us to stand there and hold Libby while she was on the phone. This meant that every day while mom was there we were tied down holding a child we did not hold all day when mom was at work. Mom then started coming an hour earlier in the afternoon and instead of picking up and leaving she would finish her workday at our house, with her car in the driveway taking up a spot needed for other parents to pick up. It got to the point where at least 2 hours a day mom was using our house as a home office and using us like mother's helpers. It became an issue one day when she came for lunch to find I had gone to Home Depot for some repairs to the house. Although my co-provider was well qualified and handling the day just fine, Libby's mom met me at the door with a demand that I never leave home again while her daughter was there. When I explained to her that the reason there were two of us and we only had 7 kids was so that we could run errands if we needed to she was not having it. When I asked if she had any reason to think her child wasn't cared for she agreed she did not. In the end I asked her for a list of accommodations she would like and I would discuss them with her. To this day I haven't received one.

This particular parent did not mean to be in anyone's way. She didn't realize what she was doing until it became a big enough problem for us to say something about it. Things are much better now, with pop-ins down to 3 a week for about thirty minutes each. She still makes us a little crazy, but we're all making progress.

THE REAL COST OF CHILDCARE

For a first time parent the cost of daycare is overwhelming. The cost of caring for one child is more than a car payment, and two kids can cost more than the mortgage. By the time you get to three it is not financially practical to work unless you are a doctor or lawyer.

Most people think that childcare providers make a killing. Centers with large numbers of children can look extremely successful while barely making ends meet. So here are the costs involved in childcare for both centers and in-home:

For Centers:

1. Payroll: this is the number one cost. Just one infant has a cost of $170 per week for staff wages and benefits. Since there is a 1*4 ratio for infants this leaves little extra for rent, utilities, toys etc.
2. Mortgage or Rent
3. Utilities
4. Commercial insurance
5. Diapers, wipes and formula
6. Groceries
7. Cleaning supplies/ Laundry
8. Toys, Books, Art Supplies
9. Tables, Chairs, Cribs
10. Transport vans and upkeep/fuel

For In-Home:

1. Provider and Co-provider's/Helper's income as well as social security, health and disability insurance and vacation pay—These are all things that are included in the staff payroll of a center.

2. Increased utility bills
3. Commercial Insurance—A good home provider will carry a daycare policy, and these are not cheap.
4. Commercial vehicle insurance—If your provider transports your child, the insurance for transporting is very pricey. It can increase their auto insurance by $300 a month, and this doesn't even account for the wear and tear on the car or the cost of gasoline.
5. Groceries—If your provider is feeding your child healthy meals the cost to feed a 3-5 year old including 2 meals and 2 snacks with milk or juice to drink is $30-$40 a week on the low side.
6. Curriculum supplies: Toys and books need replaced frequently. Art supplies are used up and have to be replenished. Google eyes, pom-poms, glitter . . . You get the picture.
7. Cleaning/laundry: Your child's blanket at daycare gets washed a lot more than at home. Everything gets scrubbed every day including washing all the toys your child played with. Try washing all your child's toys every day at home and check your water and cleaning supply bill. We go through 6 bottles of hand soap, one bottle each of Tide, Downey and Cascade dishwasher soap and 2 gallons of bleach per week in our childcare home.
8. If your provider supplies formula, diapers, wipes or baby food it adds a significant amount to the cost. Add $20 per week for diapers or formula, $10 for baby food and $2 per week for wipes.
9. Repairs to the home—Daycare is hard on a house. Spills on carpet, back door screens being run into and paint being splattered equal extra home maintenance. Parents coming in and out with salt and dirt on their shoes mean floors that need refinished or replaced much sooner than they would with just the traffic from a single family. Toilets wear out sooner being flushed by an extra 8 kids. Daycare adds at least 30% to your home maintenance costs. Just one child flushing a small dinosaur down one of our toilets caused a $400 plumbing bill, instantly adding $1 per week per child to the cost of care for an entire year.
10. Family medical—Because in-home daycare opens up their home to illness every time a daycare child comes through the door sick, the children of in-home providers and the providers themselves

have the added medical cost of a doctor's visit every time the contract one of the lovely ailments coming in courtesy of a child carrier. Last month one child gave all 8 members of my household the stomach flu. In the last 12 months we have been exposed to the flu, pink-eye, whooping cough, strep, bronchitis and impetigo as well as a weekly exposure to the common cold.

Before each child even begins childcare, the cost for supplies for that one child is a chunk of change. For each infant there is the cost of a crib, which is $200-$400. Each crib can be used for a maximum of 4 years, so only 2 infants, three at most can use that crib before it needs replaced. The mattress should be replaced every 12 months. Then there is the cost of all of the other accessories such as a swing, bouncy seat and all those silly genius toys and gizmos. So an average of $300 is spent for each new child entering daycare. This is what your deposit or enrollment fees get spent on.

Never hire a provider who charges less than everyone else around her. If she is undercutting everyone's fees and offering a deal that seems too good to be true it is usually because she cannot compete in the experience or quality department.

I will repeat a true phrase. "Find the perfect provider and then give up what you need to in order to afford her."

Summing it all up

You may think this book was written by a provider experiencing some serious burn-out. Nothing could be further from the truth. I really do love what I do. I would never have made it to 25 years without loving my job.

I love children. I smile every time I see one. I am amazed at how they learn and grow and I want to be around them all the time. I can sit with a child for hours coloring or playing with play-dough. I can talk with them about anything and laugh at the funny and insightful things they say.

Providers don't quit because they get tired of the kids. A great provider will be in love with kids their whole life. They will come to a point where the careless actions and statements of parents will take all of the joy out of childcare. It is impossible to play lightheartedly when you are worried about paying the phone bill and 2 parents haven't paid you for over a week. It is hard to be gracious to a parent who drops off a child who has obviously been medicated and expects you to just take their word for it that the fever their child has is from teething.

Parents have to understand that as providers we have the weight of the world on our shoulders. We are responsible for the health, safety and development of precious young minds and bodies. We have to protect their intelligence, their vital organs and their spirits. We must keep them safe from illness, injury and emotional damage. We must give them knowledge, a sense of self-esteem, a moral compass and more. We spend more waking hours with each child than their mother or father 5 days a week. This makes us the primary caregiver and educator. The list of our job duties is the length of a novel, and new tasks are being added daily.

When a parent violates the terms of their childcare contract it makes no difference that they have a justification or excuse. We know you need to go to work to make a living. We understand all about bills. What we cannot understand is why a spa day merits a day off but a sick child doesn't warrant 8 hours of PTO. We don't get why parents think it is impossible to take their child to the grocery store. We can't even wrap our minds around why a parent would get their child out of bed and bring them to childcare in the same sopping wet diaper they went to bed in the night before.

So here I go trying to sum it all up with a few phrases you have heard many times before but they bring everything in this book together. Here they are:

Treat us the way you would want to be treated. Speak to us with kindness and respect. We are the wise women who are shaping your child's young mind. We are the goddesses bestowing grace on your daughter, and we are the warrior teaching her she is strong and powerful. We are the nurturing force which will make your son a kind and compassionate husband and father. We are also the encouraging guides that will show him he can do anything.

Understand that we are experts in our field. Just like you revere your pediatrician, recognize that we have education, training and experience that make us qualified to give you advice. Take it when it is offered. We are simply trying to make your life easier in the long run. We are also trying to make your child the very best individual they can be. We want you to have a strong relationship with your child. We want you to be successful at parenting. We are not out to steal your child's love and affection. We are not here to make you feel bad about working. We are here to tell you that there is no quality without quantity. You cannot truly know your child spending an hour a night after work with them and then throwing them into bed early for some "me time."

Once you lie to us we find it very hard to ever trust you again. Don't do it no matter how badly you want to. If you admit your child has a temperature and ask us nicely, we may agree to take your child and keep them separate from the other kids long enough for you to go to your 10AM meeting. We will expect you to come straight back and you should only be asking as a last resort.

No matter how much we love your child, we love ours more. I can be honest about the fact that my children are the cutest, smartest and funniest in the universe. If you knowingly endanger my child I will never forget it. The parent who brought head lice into my home and just forgot to mention it still makes me irritated. The one who brought whooping cough through my door gets a slot at the top of my "If I ever go postal" list.

We need our paycheck just like you need yours. We have automatic bills that come out. We have a mortgage and a car payment. Even though we are at home we are not housewives. We are working women who work from home. The one thing I noticed was that when I ran a center parents who had paid me late constantly when I was at home all of a sudden paid their bill on time, because they saw it as a business. The only thing that had changed about their child's care was the building, but they saw it as a company, where they had seen me as a grandma figure that stayed home.

We want to be gracious. It is hard when a parent pulls up onto our grass because they don't want to wait for someone to vacate the driveway and they don't want to walk from the side street. Please observe manners and don't ruin our grass or walk in our flowerbeds. Take your shoes off at the door and don't track mud on our carpets. Leave your dog in the car PLEASE!

We want time with our family. We want to close our door at 6 PM and give our children all the attention and love you give yours when you pick them up. Please respect our family time. Be on time to pick up so that we can go home from work for the day. If there is an urgent issue we want to hear from you but we don't want a phone call asking why your child came home in a Pampers and not a Huggies. If you got home without a pacifier you don't need to call and tell us unless you are coming back to pick it up.

A lost pair of socks is not a crisis. It is fine to ask us to keep an eye out for them. It is not OK to stalk us with texts, emails and a twice daily reminder to look for them. They are on a priority list right after sanitizing the changing table and cribs, washing the nap blankets, preparing the curriculum for the next day and filling out food program forms. In other words, unless we trip over them on our way to bed we are not going to find them until we fold the 13 loads of laundry next to our bed. And that's OK. As long as we don't lose your child we are in a good place at the end of the week.

Caregivers need support. We need positive mojo to keep us singing and finger-painting with joy. When parents come through the door with constant complaints about work, the spouse, the cost of daycare or the state of the union, we have to recover mentally and emotionally after they leave. So please leave the garbage outside and help your child and your provider start the day on a lighter note. In addition please remember there is such a thing as TMI (too much information) and don't talk with us about anything you wouldn't talk about with your clients at work. We don't want to know about your sex life, your irritable bowel or your heavy drinking. If you don't want us judging you then don't give us evidence to form judgments about.

We're not ever going to talk trash about you in front of your child. Please extend us the same courtesy. Also, never talk trash to us in front of your child or ours.

Remember your provider is a human being. We are capable of making mistakes. We may not always live up to your standard. We are not perfect parents any more than you are, and our children will always save their worst behavior for when you are around. Just know that our heart is enormous, and we will work hard every day to earn your trust and respect.

It is your job to check us out. We will invite you in and answer your questions. We will let you judge our home, our kids and our personality. It is your job to do your due diligence and make sure we aren't a registered pedophile or a convicted felon. It is also your job to make sure we have a current license/registration and that we are in compliance with all of your state's laws. It is your job to check and see that our home is safe and free from hazards. It is your job to ask to see our recent training, and to make sure our CPR and First Aid certifications are current. Your employer had to check up on you and verify your education and skills set before he hired you. You are hiring someone and the job of making sure they are the right employee is yours alone. Don't just hire us based on someone else's say-so.

Once you sign up with us, remember that your parent agreement is a legal document. You have signed that you have read our wills/wont's and do's/don'ts. You agree that you will do things according to our written plan. It is like being religious, and then wanting to pick and choose which of the commandments to follow, or interpreting the scriptures so that they lean your way. The bible is fairly inflexible, and so are we.

Love your provider. Nurture and appreciate her. Buy her the occasional gift, even if it is just a new puzzle or toy for the kids. The very best gifts from parents are new toys and books for the kids. Thank your provider for all she does.

Lastly, teach your child to respect and revere their caregiver. Teach them to thank her for the little things she does for them. Help them to make gifts for her. Teach them to help out during the day and to listen and learn. Make it clear this person is in charge while you are away.

This all seems complicated but it isn't. Take your time with choosing your child's caregiver. Build a relationship based on trust and compassion. Nurture it like you do your marriage. Be willing to share your child and realize that your child is very lucky to receive love from not just 2 parents, but a co-parenting stranger who will be there whenever mom and dad can't.

Because a child can never have too many people who love him.